THE FORESTS
OF CANADA

KEN FARR

PHOTOGRAPHY BY J. DAVID ANDREWS

ADDITIONAL PHOTOGRAPHY BY

Lenard Sanders

Roberta Gal

David Barbour

Fitzhenry & Whiteside

Natural Resources Canada,

Canadian Forest Service,

Ottawa, Ontario

©Her Majesty the Queen in Right of Canada, 2003
ISBN 0-660-19004-4
Cat. no. Fo42-336/2003E

Published by Fitzhenry & Whiteside Limited, 195 Allstate Parkway, Markham, Ontario, L3R 4T8, and Natural Resources Canada, Canadian Forest Service, Ottawa, K1A 0E4, in cooperation with Public Works and Government Services Canada.

Cet ouvrage est publié en français sous le titre: *Les Forêts du Canada*.
Translation: Denis Rochon

Project Development and Research: Ken Farr
Photo Editing: Ken Farr, Sandra Bernier, and Roberta Gal
Photo Cataloguing: Francine Bérubé

Publication Management: Catherine Carmody
English Editing: Catherine Carmody and Paula Irving
Publishing Assistance: Francine Bérubé

Graphic Design: Sandra Bernier
Layout: Sandra Bernier, Julie Piché, Francine Bérubé, and Danielle Monette
Maps: Roberta Gal and Julie Piché

National Library of Canada cataloguing in publication data

Farr, Ken (Kenneth), 1954-

The forests of Canada

Issued also in French under title: Les forêts du Canada.
Co-published by: Fitzhenry & Whiteside
Includes an index.
ISBN 0-660-19004-4
Cat. no. Fo42-336/2003E

1. Forests and forestry – Canada.
I. Andrews, J. David, 1961- .
II. Canadian Forest Service.
III. Title.

SD145.F47 2003   333.75'0971   C2003-980193-4

Cover photos: *Front*, lichen-covered spruce in Fundy National Park, New Brunswick (photo by J. David Andrews); *left flap*, red alder on a coastal wetland (photo by Roberta Gal).

CONTENTS

"Nature has lavished all her grandest elements to form this astonishing panorama." (Susanna Moodie on arriving in Canada in 1832. *Roughing It in the Bush, or, Life in Canada*. Susanna Moodie. London: R. Bentley, 1852.)

PREFACE

This book celebrates, in text and images, the variety, majesty, and individual character of the forests that occur across the broad expanse of Canada, from coastal plain to mountain slopes, and from silent northern wilderness to the bustling neighborhoods of Canada's urban centers. It describes the Canadian approach to living with, caring for, managing, and enjoying forests.

There is no one typical Canadian forest. There are many forests. They differ from one region to the next and from one moment in time to the next. Each forest type is identifiable by its particular scale, composition, and aesthetic character. Each is recognized by the Canadians who live within it. The forests of Canada express the intrinsic regional variance in climate, biology, and geography that fundamentally defines Canada as a nation.

Acadian forest at sunset, Fundy National Park, New Brunswick.

About 18 000 years ago, a brief moment in geologic time, there were no forests in Canada. The landmass was almost entirely covered by an immense blanket of shifting, glacial ice, in places 2 km deep. Advancing glaciers had crushed and removed most of the vegetation, exposing the bare rock of the Precambrian Shield. They had carved out the steep-walled valleys that now exist between western mountain ranges and deposited the sands, gravels, tills, and clays that underlie much of Canada's present vegetation.

The conifers of the Pacific coast, the pines and spruces of the boreal forest, and the maples and oaks of the eastern broadleaf forests were absent from this land. They refuged farther south, in Washington, Oregon, Kansas, Nebraska, Kentucky, Georgia, Tennessee, and Florida. There, they waited out the long glacial winter, which eventually gave way to an interglacial spring.

The first land to emerge from the ice was Canada's most southerly point, the peninsula of southwestern Ontario. By 14 000 years ago, it was a treeless, subarctic tundra dotted with isolated patches of spruce forest. A thousand years later, a closed-canopy conifer forest began to develop. This gave way to a mix of pine, hemlock, and broadleaf species by 11 000 years ago and then to oak, beech, elms, and maples 3000 years later.

The glaciers retreated from the Maritime provinces around 11 000 years ago and a forest of spruce and birch began its invasion from the southwest.

Coastal British Columbia started to unfreeze later than the east coast, but by 7000 years ago the lower mainland coast was an open-canopy forest of pines and Douglas-fir. Another thousand years saw the development of western hemlock and western redcedar as the dominant species and the emergence of a temperate rainforest.

In northern Quebec and Labrador, the last residual continental ice caps had disappeared by 6000 years ago; a vanguard forest of spruce and fir reached the region 2000 years later. Only 3000 years ago, the boreal forest had made its maximum northerly advance. Since that time, failing to regenerate after wildfires, it has retreated southward about 300 km.

Today, Canada is almost half-covered in forest, 4.2 million km² from coast to coast. In southwestern Ontario, the first area to emerge after the ice, the diverse broadleaf cover includes a last wave of southern arboreal travelers, cucumber magnolias, black tupelos, sassafras, and redbud. But if you look here and there, tucked in kettle bogs and low-lying wetlands, small stands of black spruce remain, possible relics of the very first postglacial forest to reclaim the land that would become Canada.

Perhaps no country has been so influenced by forests as Canada. Its history, pattern of development, and economic status have, for 400 years, been directly influenced by forests. Many Canadian towns and cities, including Ottawa, the nation's

OPPOSITE This pictograph, or rock painting, in Farwell Canyon, British Columbia, attests to the long cultural and spiritual heritage of Canada's First Nations.

Transporting square timber on a Quebec river in the nineteenth century.

capital, came into being and are located where they are because of an imperative to access, transport, manufacture, and export forest resources. Canada's history is the history of its forests.

From early times, Canadians have exploited the forests around them. Aboriginal peoples harvested trees to build houses, make canoes, and fashion a wide range of implements for hunting, fishing, and farming. Their relationship with the forest was based on cultural and spiritual values and this directly influenced the composition and distribution of the forests.

The arrival of Europeans in North America resulted in a significant increase in forest resource exploitation. The colonial population in Canada was tiny, and settlement involved clearing modest areas of forest to support agriculture. Any wood harvested was chiefly for individual use as building material or fuel. Until the mid-eighteenth century, forest exploitation and management was mostly limited to a subsistence level.

Throughout the eighteenth and nineteenth centuries, colonial growth was accompanied by a rapid rise in the commercial trading of forest resources. The harvesting of timber during this era lacked any form of organized management. Wood was the perfect resource for the age. It floated and could be easily transported by river from inland to seaport. It was used to build the ships needed to transport it to Europe and which would carry settlers to North America on the return journey. In the early nineteenth century, timber from the forests of eastern Canada took on new importance. Eastern white pine, the largest tree species by height or volume in eastern North America, was central to this new era of large-scale forest exploitation. Its harvesting for the square timber trade with Britain supported provincial economies and enabled the establishment of resource-based Canadian industries. Keeping pace with a growing Canadian population, the forest industry constructed mills that relied on timber obtained from land cleared for settlement and from lands completely dedicated to the harvesting of timber. Along Canada's Pacific coast, timber exploitation on this scale occurred somewhat later, in the mid-nineteenth century.

In the latter part of the nineteenth century, widespread concern over the scale and sustainability of white pine harvesting in eastern Canada led directly to the creation of a federal forestry service. This agency, which in time was to become the Canadian Forest Service, was created to oversee the "preservation of timber on Dominion lands and carry out policies to encourage tree culture in districts already open to settlement." Provincial governments began to develop agencies for overseeing timber cutting. Forest conservation, protection, and propagation were becoming issues.

From the 1920s until the 1960s, forest management in Canada continued to evolve. As Canada developed into an urbanized, industrial society, the forest resource industry grew rapidly. Provincial governments granted long-term forest management licenses to ensure a steady wood supply. Sustained-yield management had become the primary approach.

During the 1960s and 1970s, Canada's forest resource industry grew as Canadian lumber and paper products were exported to a global marketplace. Concurrently, Canadians became more affluent and had more available leisure time. They were demanding access to forest lands for hunting, fishing, and other recreational pursuits. Forest managers now had to adopt forest management strategies aimed at multiple uses of forests.

Throughout the 1970s and 1980s, multiple-use forest management evolved into integrated resource management. Wildlife, hydrology and water quality, integrated pest management systems, nontimber values, and a wider range of forest products and land uses were considered in managing Canada's forests. Managers, scientists, and technicians worked together, applying a wide range of skills to develop forest management plans.

From the 1990s to the present, forest management in Canada has undergone profound changes in its objectives and philosophy. The sustainable management of forest resources has become an ultimate goal and a yardstick against which effective

TOP Proud loggers pose with a champion load of 110 logs on a single sled, Whitefish River, Ontario, 1891.

BOTTOM A woman working in British Columbia's coastal forest in 1943 uses a peavey to move a log.

TOP Innovative forestry often begins with research carried out in laboratories across Canada. Deborah Buhlers in a Canadian Forest Service greenhouse.

BOTTOM Precise planning of harvests and specialized equipment are an important part of forest management in Canada.

forest management practices are to be measured. Canada's provinces have amended legislation to ensure recognition of the diverse uses and multiple benefits forests provide to all Canadians. As steward to 10% of the world's forest resources, Canada is committed to demonstrating global leadership in forest management by maintaining the biological diversity, ecological vitality, and extent of its forests, for the cultural and economic needs of all Canadians, and for the citizens of the world.

Innovation, Partnership, and Global Stewardship

Canada's approach to its forests is encompassed in a commitment to sustainable forest management. This commitment has been clearly expressed in the National Forest Strategy and in the Canada Forest Accord. The expressed goal of these documents is to maintain and enhance the long-term health of Canadian forest ecosystems for the benefit of all living things, both nationally and globally, while providing environmental, economic, social, and cultural opportunities for the benefit of present and future generations.

Community stewardship and participation are critical factors in developing and testing new approaches to forest management. Implementation of innovative programs that encourage partnerships and develop capacity, such as Canada's Model Forest Program, is one way of doing this. Dedicated to the achievement of sustainable forest management, the Model Forest Program is a network of 11 forests across Canada.

Model forests serve to increase forest knowledge and bring people together to develop solutions to the complex challenges of sustainable forest management. Community and Aboriginal groups, governments, industry, researchers, and nongovernmental organizations together find practical solutions to management problems. Canada's model forests support research in science and technology development and promote social, environmental, and economic sustainability.

Another innovative approach to forest management is Canada's First Nations Forestry Program, which assists and supports First Nations in managing their forest resources and promotes economic development and employment opportunities. Increasingly, forests have become an important economic resource for First Nations communities, the majority of which are located in productive forest areas across Canada. First Nations actively participate in managing, directing, and implementing the program.

Canada has also demonstrated its commitment to forest stewardship and sustainable forest management practices on the international stage. In 1992, at the United Nations Conference on Environment and Development in Rio de Janeiro, Brazil, Canada was among more than a hundred countries that signed the Convention on Biological Diversity, one of the first industrialized countries to ratify the convention.

In addition, Canada is a participant in the Montréal Process, an initiative launched among non-European temperate and boreal countries to develop and

implement criteria and indicators for sustainable forest management. In 1995, Canada and 11 other forest nations agreed on a set of 7 criteria and 67 associated indicators.

Canadian technology, such as the Bombardier 415 amphibious water bomber, has advanced forest management in Canada and around the world.

Forest Science and Technology

Canada has seen its forest science and technology capacity advance from conducting forest resource surveys on horseback to measuring forest cover by satellite. Amphibious water-bombers often lend support to or supplant on-the-ground fire suppression efforts, while forest fire images and statistics are sent instantaneously across the country by the Internet. For more than a hundred years, Canada's federal and provincial forest research organizations, universities, industrial research institutes, networks of excellence, and industry have produced world-class science aimed at improving the management and condition of forests.

Canada's forests can be broadly categorized as follows: 67% is coniferous (often called softwood), composed of genera such as spruce, pine, and fir; 15% is primarily broadleaf (also referred to as hardwood or deciduous), composed of genera such as maple, ash, and oak; and 18% has more or less equal numbers of conifer and broadleaf species (referred to as mixedwood). Canada's forests contain 10 genera and 31 species of native conifers and 50 genera and 149 species of native broadleaf trees.

Formerly forest research focused on the operational aspects of forest management, thus helping to protect forest resources and increase fiber production. This work continues, but researchers are also seeking answers to basic questions about forest productivity, landscape management, natural disturbance processes, and ecosystem-based forest management.

Canada's future science and technology capacity will need to focus on new and emerging challenges, including mitigating the effects on forests of climate change, monitoring forest biodiversity, measuring forest carbon storage, improving wood quality, developing faster growing trees, and creating automated forest monitoring and inventory systems. Maintaining a cutting-edge capacity in forest science and technology is and will continue to be an important aspect of Canada's approach to its forests.

The forest types described in this book are based on a system of describing forests developed by W.E.D. Halliday in 1937 and later refined by J.S. Rowe in a map (1959) and publication (1972).[1] This system is known as Forest Regions of Canada. Forest regions are major geographic zones characterized by distinct combinations of dominant tree species. There are eight forest regions: the Acadian in the Maritimes; the Great Lakes–St. Lawrence in central Canada; the Deciduous in southwestern Ontario; the Boreal stretching across Canada's north; the Subalpine and the Montane in Alberta and British Columbia; and the Columbia and the Coast in British Columbia. Collectively, they give a complete geographic description of Canada's forests.

Many systems of classification exist for regions, countries, continents, and even the earth. An ecological land classification system, Ecozones of Canada, is now widely accepted for Canada.[2] Ecozones define, on a subcontinental scale, the broad mosaics formed by the interaction of climate, human activity, vegetation, soils, and geologic and physiographic features of the country.

Because Forest Regions of Canada focuses exclusively on forests, it has been chosen as the simpler alternative for structuring the descriptions of forests in this publication. However, the word "region" is omitted (for example, Acadian Forest Region is Acadian forest); "Deciduous" has been replaced by "Carolinian"; and "Coast" becomes "coastal". In addition, another forest type has been included— the forest preserved or created within Canada's urban areas—because for many Canadians, this is the forest where a day-to-day relationship with trees takes place.

Descriptions in the text include values for mean annual, summer, and winter temperatures and for mean annual precipitation. These climatic measurements are seasonal averages for broad areas. They do not capture short-term changes in climate or variation for specific locations, but do allow general comparisons of forest types.

Note also that only the common names of organisms appear in the text; a list of scientific names is on page 145.

---

[1] *Forest Regions of Canada*. Publication No. 1300. Department of the Environment, Canadian Forestry Service, 1972.

[2] A National Ecological Framework for Canada. Ecological Stratification Working Group, 1996. http://sis.agr.gc.ca/cansis/publications/ecostrat/intro.html.

TOP A coniferous forest in northern Saskatchewan.

MIDDLE A broadleaf forest in southern Ontario.

BOTTOM A mixedwood forest in New Brunswick.

FOREST TYPES

ACADIAN FOREST
Red spruce, balsam fir, maple, yellow birch

COASTAL FOREST
Western redcedar, western hemlock, Sitka spruce, Douglas-fir

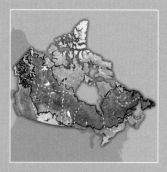

BOREAL FOREST
White spruce, black spruce, balsam fir, jack pine, white birch, trembling aspen, tamarack, willow

COLUMBIA FOREST
Western redcedar, western hemlock, Douglas-fir

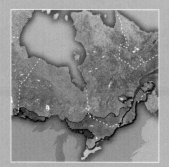

GREAT LAKES–ST. LAWRENCE FOREST
Red pine, eastern white pine, eastern hemlock, yellow birch, maple, oak

MONTANE FOREST
Douglas-fir, lodgepole pine, ponderosa pine, trembling aspen

CAROLINIAN FOREST
Beech, maple, black walnut, hickory, oak

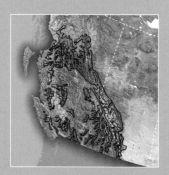

SUBALPINE FOREST
Engelmann spruce, subalpine fir, lodgepole pine

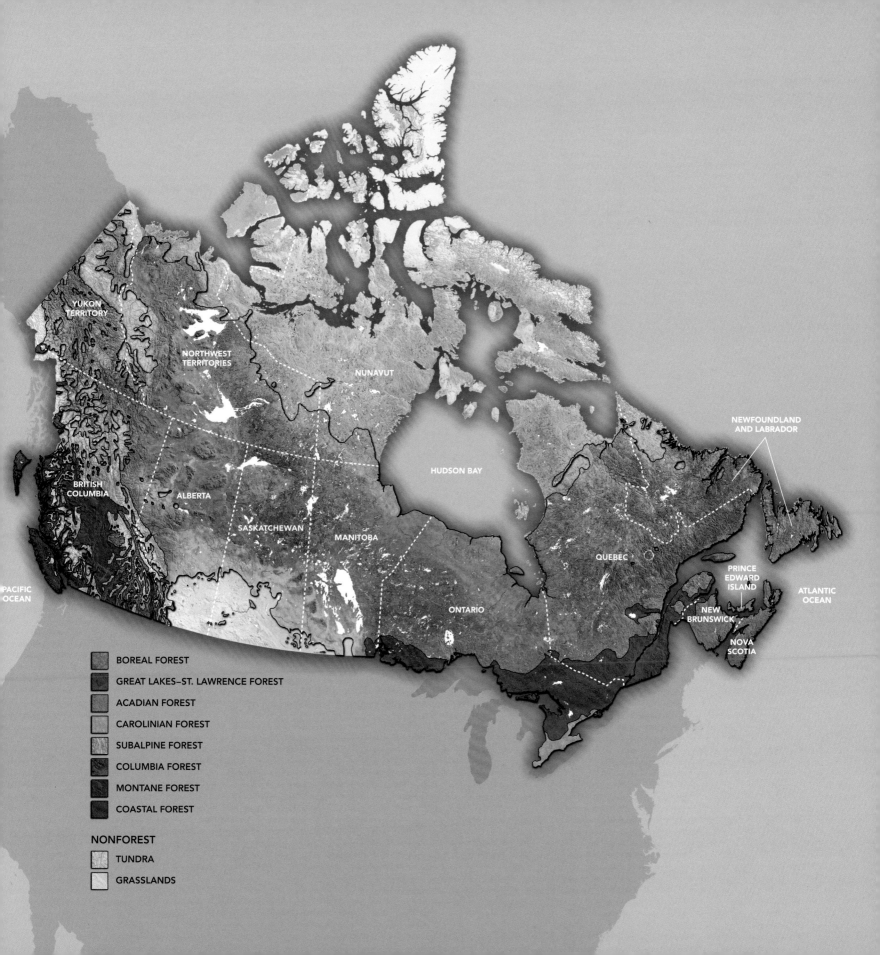

YUKON
TERRITORY

NORTHWEST
TERRITORIES

NUNAVUT

BRITISH
COLUMBIA

ALBERTA

SASKATCHEWAN

MANITOBA

HUDSON BAY

NEWFOUNDLAND
AND LABRADOR

QUEBEC

ONTARIO

PRINCE
EDWARD
ISLAND

NEW
BRUNSWICK

NOVA
SCOTIA

PACIFIC
OCEAN

ATLANTIC
OCEAN

BOREAL FOREST

GREAT LAKES–ST. LAWRENCE FOREST

ACADIAN FOREST

CAROLINIAN FOREST

SUBALPINE FOREST

COLUMBIA FOREST

MONTANE FOREST

COASTAL FOREST

NONFOREST

TUNDRA

GRASSLANDS

ACADIAN
FOREST

400 years after European settlement, the Acadian forest remains ecologically distinct

On Canada's east coast, the Acadian forest forms a transition zone between the predominantly spruce and pine boreal forest to the north and the largely broadleaf forests of the northeastern United States. Although the Acadian forest represents only 2.2% of the total forest area of Canada, it is a forest area of striking variety. The Acadian forest occupies 91 290 km^2, covering nearly all of Nova Scotia and Prince Edward Island and the southern two-thirds of New Brunswick.

Like the Great Lakes–St. Lawrence forest to the west, the Acadian forest features a broad mix of conifer and broadleaf tree species. However, because of the moderating influence of the Atlantic Ocean and the effects of local topography, the Acadian forest also presents a unique and recognizable mix of plant species. Landforms in the forest range from tidal inlets, sand dunes, and swampy lowlands to soaring cliffs and rugged, inhospitable, rocky plateaus. At seaside locations or on exposed highlands, prevailing sea winds directly influence the growth and form of the forest stands.

Fog-shrouded forest around Wolfe Lake, New Brunswick.

Much of the Acadian forest enjoys a moderate and stable ocean climate. Away from the ocean's direct influence, however, winters can be cold and very snowy. Annual precipitation ranges between 900 and 1400 mm inland, increasing closer to the coast. Summers range from cool to warm and moist, with mean temperatures between 14° and 15.5°C. During winter, mean temperatures throughout much of the forest range from −2.5° to −5.5°C.

In areas such as the Saint John River valley, the forest is predominantly broadleaf and features rich mixed stands. In the highlands of north-central New Brunswick and on the highest points of the Cape Breton highlands, little more than dwarf birch occurs, which is replaced at higher elevations by moss and heath barrens. The mean temperatures at these elevations is −8.0°C in winter, and the season is long, snowy, and cold.

The variety of plant species in the Acadian forest stems from a confluence of plant communities found nowhere else in Canada: remnant arctic and alpine plants

March thaw along the Little Tobique River, Mount Carleton Provincial Park, New Brunswick.

TOP Spruce seedlings and leaves of red maple add color to the forest floor.

BOTTOM In the moist maritime climate, mosses and fungi form thick carpets.

RIGHT Old-growth yellow and white birch, Fundy Model Forest, New Brunswick.

from the retreat of the glaciers, plants of the coastal plain of the Atlantic seaboard, assemblages of northerly species from the boreal forest, and communities from the Appalachian mountain chains to the southwest. In Nova Scotia alone, more than 200 plant species are considered rare. The majority of these are common elsewhere in their distribution, but occur in the Acadian forest at the very northern edge of their natural range. Nine species—mountain avens, New Jersey rush, pink tickseed, threadleaf sundew, goldencrest, Plymouth rose gentian, sweet pepperbush, water pennywort, and eastern grasswort—are classified either as endangered, threatened, or of special concern in Canada.

Despite its diversity, the Acadian forest contains no tree species that cannot be found elsewhere in Canada. Red spruce, a long-living shade-tolerant tree, is the most characteristic species. Eastern white pine, red pine, jack pine, balsam fir, eastern hemlock, and Canada yew are other common conifers.

Mountain paper birch and gray birch are characteristic early succession species, rapidly filling gaps after forest disturbance. Sugar maple, American beech, and yellow birch, together in various combinations, form a major component of the Acadian forest. Other commonly encountered broadleaf trees include red maple, white ash, red ash, black ash, red oak, ironwood, largetooth aspen, and black cherry. A few species that are generally common farther west in Canada are uncommon or even rare in the Acadian forest. These include silver maple, butternut, bur oak, basswood, black willow, and Canada plum, each of which occurs at a few locations in New Brunswick.

Several small tree and shrub species typical of the Great Lakes–St. Lawrence and the Carolinian forests reach the northeastern limits of their range in the Acadian forest, including alternate-leaf dogwood, round-leaf dogwood, mountain maple, striped maple, witch-hazel, common winterberry, staghorn sumac, American elder, and beaked hazel. Others, such as northern bayberry, are typical of the shoreline ecosystems of the eastern United States and only just reach into Canada in the Acadian forest.

The Acadian forest provides habitat for wildlife species typical of the boreal, Great Lakes–St. Lawrence, and Carolinian forests. Characteristic mammals include American pine marten, moose, American black bear, red fox, snowshoe hare, North American porcupine, fisher, American beaver, bobcat, muskrat, and raccoon.

Common birds are the great blue heron, Lincoln's sparrow, bay-breasted warbler, yellow-bellied sapsucker, rough-legged hawk, and American golden-plover. Amphibians and reptiles include the eastern painted turtle, wood turtle, gray treefrog, blue-spotted salamander, spring peeper, ringneck snake, and smooth green snake.

The term "Acadian" is derived from *Acadie*, the name given to this area by the early French settlers. This was the first forest area in Canada to be extensively explored and settled, and over the centuries, successive waves of forest resource alteration and use have occurred. Large parts of the area were long ago cleared for settlement and agriculture.

The Acadian forest was the initial source of eastern white pine square timber for Great Britain, which needed wood to rebuild her merchant marine and navy in the early nineteenth century. Thus also began the domestic timber trade in British

North America. So considerable was the level of forest exploitation that repeated and widespread wildfires fueled by logging debris occurred. The result was a less extensive forest with fewer species. In particular, repeated fires favored tree species that were quick to regenerate on burnt-over sites, eventually producing even-aged conifer stands in place of the original mixed forests.

Only about 5% of the original Acadian forest remains, limited to the most inaccessible locations and rugged, high elevation sites. The contemporary forest is, however, highly productive. Much of the forest has repeatedly regenerated following harvesting. As well, farms and homesteads established on marginal lands and subsequently abandoned have returned to a forest state. Nearly 88 170 km^2, or 96.6% of the Acadian forest, is currently classified as timber-productive land.

Natural forest disturbances tend to be localized in the Acadian forest. A process of constant, incremental small-scale change, referred to as gap disturbance, is driven by extreme wind events, disease, and periodic insect infestations. The process creates small

Lichen-covered spruce in Fundy National Park, New Brunswick.

Tamarack favor swampy lowlands.

areas and openings in the established forest canopy, where young shade-tolerant trees compete with short-lived pioneer species. As a result, the Acadian forest tends to develop stable assemblages of long-lived trees such as sugar maple, red spruce, and yellow birch.

Large-scale disturbances in the Acadian forest, such as fire, take place in areas where forest composition has shifted to extensive jack pine and white spruce stands. Close to the Atlantic coast, forest stands are affected by prevailing ocean winds and the desiccating effects of salt spray, producing unique landscapes of stunted balsam fir and white spruce.

Resources provided by the Acadian forest are important to the local and provincial economy. More than half of the Acadian forest is privately owned, rather than crown-owned, unlike Canada's other forests. In addition to extensive pulp and paper and lumber industries, the forest supports numerous small-scale Christmas tree and maple syrup enterprises. In the year 2001, more than 1 million Christmas trees and about 1.5 million litres of maple syrup were exported from the area.

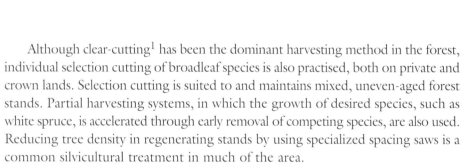

Although clear-cutting[1] has been the dominant harvesting method in the forest, individual selection cutting of broadleaf species is also practised, both on private and crown lands. Selection cutting is suited to and maintains mixed, uneven-aged forest stands. Partial harvesting systems, in which the growth of desired species, such as white spruce, is accelerated through early removal of competing species, are also used. Reducing tree density in regenerating stands by using specialized spacing saws is a common silvicultural treatment in much of the area.

At present, rising demand for forest resources in the Acadian forest has resulted in allocation of nearly all of the fiber resource available for harvest. Finding ways to

LEFT Autumn scene near Blue Bell Lake, New Brunswick.

RIGHT Dickson Falls, New Brunswick.

PAGE 28 A mixed forest of spruce, pine, maple, beech, and oak.

PAGE 29 Tangled branches of mountain-ash frame a background of autumn color.

[1] Clear-cutting, in the Canadian context, is the simultaneous harvest of most merchantable trees in a stand. This approach is normally taken in stands that develop after natural disturbances such as fire. Clear-cutting often includes retention of some mature trees to act as a seed source, which accelerates reforestation of the harvested site.

TOP Laura Folkins gathering white pine boughs to make decorative wreaths, Kierstead Mountain, New Brunswick.

BOTTOM Fashioning a traditional Maliseet basket from black ash, Victor Bear of the Tobique First Nation.

RIGHT Canadian Forest Service researchers Ron Smith and Stewart Cameron are developing propagation techniques for Canada yew.

protect the forest from insects, diseases, and wildfire is of critical concern to forest researchers and managers. Its location near the ocean and thus international seaports makes the forest especially vulnerable to alien invasive pests. Preventing their establishment and controlling existing invasions are major research areas.

Current research in the forest also focuses on establishment of criteria and indicators of sustainable forest practices, certification of sustainable forest management practices, improvement of forest management on private lands, and efforts to ensure the long-term viability of bur oak, butternut, and white elm populations.

The Acadian forest plays an important socioeconomic role in the lives of its residents. Researchers are studying and quantifying the contribution of nontimber resources such as recreation, camping, fishing, and ecotourism to local economies. As well, other economic sources are being explored: maple syrup production; the harvesting of conifer boughs, particularly those of balsam fir and white pine, for decorative wreaths; the cropping of wild blueberries; and the propagation of Canada

yew, which contains substances called taxanes that show potential for the treatment of some cancers.

The Acadian forest contains two model forests, the Fundy Model Forest in New Brunswick and the Nova Forest Alliance in Nova Scotia. The Fundy Model Forest, 4200 km^2 of Acadian forest in southern New Brunswick, has 34 diverse partners representing the federal and provincial governments, Aboriginal organizations, the forest industry, regional private woodlot owners, and environmental groups. The Nova Forest Alliance has a land base of 4580 km^2 in central Nova Scotia and is made up of small private landowners, pulp and lumber companies, municipalities, community groups, and all levels of government.

The forest encompasses numerous provincial parks and five national parks: Fundy National Park and Kouchibouguac National Park in New Brunswick; Prince Edward Island National Park in Prince Edward Island; and Kejimkujik National Park and Cape Breton Highlands National Park in Nova Scotia.

TOP Dale Simpson holds samples from the Canadian Forest Service's National Tree Seed Centre in Fredericton, New Brunswick.

BOTTOM Seeds of sugar maple, red spruce, eastern white-cedar, and speckled alder collected in the Acadian forest.

TOP A late-winter storm on Folly Mountain, Nova Scotia.

BOTTOM Winters can be cold and snowy in parts of the Acadian forest.

RIGHT White birch stand in Kouchibouguac National Park, New Brunswick.

The Acadian forest has changed in the 400 years since European contact. Today, it is more uniform in species composition, younger, and more even-aged. However, it has maintained its ecological distinctness and continues to exhibit qualities that distinguish it as a unique forest type.

Deep snows help to insulate these spruce seedlings in the Cobequid Mountains of Nova Scotia.

BOREAL
FOREST

*Canada's most extensive forest type, the boreal forest
is part of the largest terrestrial ecosystem on earth*

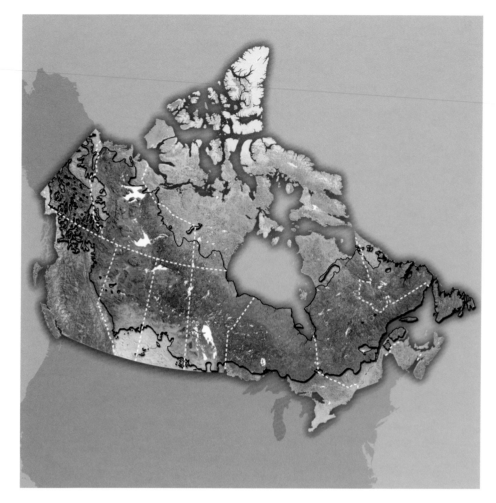

PRECEDING PAGES Aurora borealis illuminates boreal forest along the Notikewin River near Manning, Alberta.

BELOW Scattered spruce along the Thelon River mark the boreal forest's northern limit in the barrens of Nunavut.

In Canada's north, a vast conifer forest of narrow-crowned pines, firs, and spruces extends unbroken from one side of the continent to the other. The boreal forest is larger than all other Canadian forest types combined. It occupies over 3.2 million km^2, or 77% of the total forest area of Canada. Extending from the northwestern border of the Yukon Territory to the most eastern tip of Newfoundland, it is part of a forest complex that circles the globe, stretching across North America, Europe, and Asia, forming the largest terrestrial ecosystem on earth.

The most northern part of the boreal forest in Canada is in the Northwest Territories, where a barren and scattered forest extends to nearly 70° north latitude, in the area of the Mackenzie River delta. The boreal tree line stretches southeast in a great arc, meandering through the Northwest Territories and Nunavut, reaching the western shore of Hudson Bay about 150 km north of Churchill, Manitoba. East of Hudson Bay, it continues in a northeastern arc, across Quebec and Labrador, reaching as far north as 57° north latitude at the shore of Ungava Bay in the eastern

Atlantic Ocean. Throughout much of this range, the boreal tree line forms an uneven transitional zone between forest and tundra, moving in response to changes in climatic extremes and the location and frequency of wildfires.

    At its most northern extent, the boreal forest consists of scattered conifer stands and areas of sprawling willow and alder shrubs interrupting arctic tundra. The ground is covered by various species of lichens that establish quickly after fire and are highly efficient at accessing the limited moisture and nutrient content available. On cold barren sites, particularly after fire, the thick lichen mat inhibits the establishment of tree species, maintaining a scattered, open-canopy forest.

    Farther south, where climatic conditions are more favorable, there is an extensive zone of thick conifer forest. Supplemented by broadleaf tree species that can rapidly colonize after fire, the boreal forest here is rich and highly productive. Beneath the closed canopy, the ground cover is a complex and varied mix of moss, lichen, and herbaceous plant species.

White spruce in a valley along the Dempster Highway, Yukon Territory.

Black spruce glisten in the pale winter sun,
Parc national des Grands-Jardins, Quebec.

TOP The Cypress Hills form isolated islands of boreal forest in the grasslands of southern Saskatchewan and Alberta.

BOTTOM Canadian Forest Service researcher Cecilia Feng investigates harvesting impacts on water temperature and evaporation in the boreal forest.

RIGHT Scientists are conducting a large-scale experiment on this site near Peace River, Alberta, to determine whether forest management techniques can mimic natural disturbances.

The boreal forest changes in character again in southern Alberta, Saskatchewan, and Manitoba. Adjacent to the prairie grasslands, the closed-canopy conifer forest gradually transforms into an open area of scattered stands. These stands are replaced by extensive groves of trembling aspen. The line between forest and grassland changes in response to climatic extremes, and throughout southern Saskatchewan and central Alberta, isolated islands of aspen and boreal conifer forest dot the grasslands.

The southern boundary of the boreal forest traces an irregular, meandering path westward through north-central British Columbia, touching the coastal forest at its northern frontier. It follows the eastern slope of the Rocky Mountains where it merges with the subalpine forest. From southeastern Manitoba and Lake Superior, eastward through Ontario and Quebec to the Gulf of St. Lawrence, the boreal forest marks the northern limit of the Great Lakes–St. Lawrence forest, and the two forest types overlap and share species. In Quebec, two isolated sections of boreal forest exist on the central Gaspé peninsula, surrounded by Great Lakes–St. Lawrence forest. Farther east, Anticosti Island in the Gulf of St. Lawrence and Newfoundland and Labrador are exclusively boreal forest.

The boreal forest extends across a wide range of landforms. In the Northwest Territories, it grows on flat terrain, in deep river canyons, and over discontinuous permafrost. It occupies mountainous highlands and covers plains in the southern Yukon and northern British Columbia and then crosses the flat prairie terrain of northern Alberta and Saskatchewan. In the area surrounding Hudson Bay and western James Bay, the boreal landscape includes boggy, wet forest, or muskeg, moss and lichen tundra, and raised coastal beaches. Across Nunavut, northern Manitoba and Quebec, Labrador, and north-central Ontario and Quebec, the boreal forest covers the vast ancient bedrock of the Precambrian Shield.

Climate across the boreal forest is as variable as the landforms it covers. At its coastal extremes, conditions are moderated by maritime influences. On the Avalon Peninsula of eastern Newfoundland, the mean winter temperature is −1°C and the mean annual precipitation 1400–1500 mm. At inland locations, such as the Peace River Lowlands in northern Alberta, the climate is continental. The mean winter temperature is −14°C and mean annual precipitation is only 350–600 mm.

Climatic variation has a major impact on forest succession in the boreal forest. Wildfire is the critical ecological disturbance for most of the forest, occurring at more or less regular intervals and maintaining even-aged forests dominated by conifer species. Near the coasts, where humid, maritime conditions prevail, fire is much less frequent. As a result, forest trees live longer and fire is replaced as a disturbance by insects, diseases, and windstorms.

Despite an expanse of continental scale, the boreal forest has a remarkably uniform appearance and character. Throughout the forest, five conifer species dominate the landscape. White spruce is common on well-drained upland sites. Black spruce dominates low, wet sites, though it is also able to colonize quick-draining upland areas. Balsam fir is widespread in eastern Canada, especially where maritime conditions prevail, and ranges westward as far as north-central Alberta. Jack pine, a species particularly

Almost half (1.8 million km²) of Canada's forest area is noncommercial. It is largely wilderness. Remote and composed of small, scattered slow-growing trees, it is not sufficiently productive to make it economically worthwhile to harvest. Of the 56% of Canada's forest land that is classified as commercial, about half (1.2 million km²) is managed for timber production. The remainder is inaccessible or unavailable for harvesting under policy constraints, which include provisions for reserves, watercourse buffers, and protected areas.

adept at colonizing sites burned by wildfire, is present throughout almost all of the boreal forest, most often colonizing quick-draining sandy sites. Tamarack, the boreal forest's only deciduous conifer, is also present throughout the forest, except in the far northwest. Best adapted to moist soils and ample sunlight, it often grows to the edge of northern fens and bogs. In western Canada, where the boreal forest merges with the subalpine forest, balsam fir is replaced by subalpine fir, and jack pine intergrades and hybridizes with lodgepole pine.

Several broadleaf tree species, highly adapted to harsh conditions and frequent fires, occur in the forest. All have extensive ranges, and all are pioneer species, quick to establish on well-drained, burnt-over sites. The ubiquitous trembling aspen produces and stores more aboveground biomass than any other tree. Trembling aspen is particularly well adapted to a harsh winter climate; it has a special sublayer of chlorophyll-producing bark that allows it to photosynthesize in a limited way even without leaves. Balsam poplar is almost as widely distributed as trembling aspen.

Trembling aspen advancing at the edge of open grasslands.

White birch is also common, although distinctive genetic populations in the eastern and northwestern sections of its range may be interpreted as separate species. Willow species, including pussy willow, Bebb willow, and shining willow, are widespread and most often found on poorly drained sites. Speckled and green alder are common lowland species throughout the forest.

Common herbs and grasses of the boreal forest include round-leaf sundew, purple pitcherplant, American twinflower, wild sarsaparilla, fireweed, fragrant bedstraw, blue-joint reedgrass, and tall cotton-grass. Common shrubs include several species of cranberry and blueberry, Saskatoon-berry, northern meadowsweet, russet buffaloberry, kinnikinnick (bearberry), Canadian bunchberry, bog-laurel, and bog Labrador-tea. More than 40 species of mosses, characteristically sphagnum species, occur throughout the boreal forest. They are the most dominant life-form of the forest, blanketing forest floors and covering open bogs and muskeg in layers thick enough to support trees. Lichens are the primary winter food of caribou.

Characteristic mammals of the boreal forest include the American black bear, caribou, moose, white-tailed deer, gray wolf, and American beaver. Common bird species include the boreal chickadee, great gray owl, pine grosbeak, spruce grouse, white-throated sparrow, and gray jay. In the southern and central portions of the forest, a few reptile and amphibian species are found, including the five-lined skink, common garter snake, eastern fox snake, northern water snake, boreal chorus frog, northern leopard frog, wood frog, common snapping turtle, and spotted turtle.

Until the early twentieth century, the remoteness of the boreal forest and the relatively small size of its component trees had restricted forest harvesting and forest management activities. Over the last 50 years, however, world demand for pulp, paper, and wood products has steadily risen, consequently increasing the use and allocation of boreal forest resources. In addition to timber, demand has increased for oil and gas, minerals, metals, and hydroelectric power generation, which all affect the boreal forest.

LEFT The great gray owl ranges throughout the boreal forest.

RIGHT On the dry southern prairies, tree growth is limited to the edges of streams and bogs.

Wetlands are a biologically rich part of the boreal forest.

TOP A bear has left claw marks in the smooth bark of this trembling aspen.

BOTTOM The fruit of Canadian bunchberry is an important source of food for boreal wildlife.

RIGHT Forest floor near Namekus Lake, Prince Albert National Park, Saskatchewan.

Established after a wildfire, this 25-year-old trembling aspen stand provides shelter for regenerating white spruce.

About 1.6 million km², or 51.7%, of the boreal forest is classified as timber-productive land. The boreal forest is an important component of the Canadian forest resource sector and a major contributor to the Canadian economy. While clear-cutting has been the most frequently used silvicultural system, development of low-impact harvesting techniques and other silvicultural alternatives is ongoing. Also employed are two-stage silvicultural systems that allow harvest of a mature crop while simultaneously protecting an immature understory for future use. The maximum size of harvest sites is regulated throughout the boreal forest, and it is generally required that buffer strips of uncut trees be retained to protect watercourses, wildlife habitat, and sensitive areas.

Currently, researchers are investigating the primary productivity and forest biodiversity of the boreal forest to better describe its ecosystem functions. Canada's ability to monitor and predict wildfires and outbreaks of insects and diseases has increased dramatically in recent years. Researchers are now studying the effects of

Over 40 species of mosses occur in the boreal forest, often blanketing the forest floor.

This burned site near La Ronge, Saskatchewan, demonstrates the rejuvenating effect of wildfire in the boreal forest.

TOP Natural disturbances and harvesting create a patchwork of forest stands.

BOTTOM In mixed stands of trembling aspen, birch, balsam fir, and white spruce, the aging broadleaf species in the upper canopy shelter the younger conifers below.

RIGHT Machine operator Randall Charrette, part of a private logging operation managed in cooperation with the Canadian Forest Service, north of Athabasca, Alberta.

these disturbances to better emulate nature when harvesting boreal stands. The Canadian Forest Service is a partner in one such project—Ecosystem Management by Emulating Natural Disturbance, or EMEND. A large-scale fire-ecology experiment in northwestern Alberta, EMEND covers nearly 12 km² of boreal forest and is scheduled to take place over a hundred years.

Of global importance are research efforts in the boreal forest to determine the relationships between projected climate change and the ability of this vast region to act as either a sink or source for atmospheric carbon.[1]

For Canadians and international visitors, the forest's countless remote lakes, rivers, and wilderness settings have become highly valued places of solitude and outdoor recreation. To protect and preserve the biodiversity and wild character

[1] A forest in which carbon stocks are increasing is called a sink; one in which carbon stocks are decreasing, a source.

of the boreal forest, Canada has created 11 national parks and reserves within its boundaries. They are Nahanni National Park Reserve and Wood Buffalo National Park in the Northwest Territories; Elk Island National Park in Alberta; Prince Albert National Park in Saskatchewan; Wapusk and Riding Mountain national parks in Manitoba; Pukaskwa National Park in Ontario; Mingan Archipelago National Park Reserve and Forillon National Park in Quebec; and Gros Morne and Terra Nova national parks in Newfoundland and Labrador. Provincial parks within the boreal forest are located in Newfoundland and Labrador, Quebec, Ontario, Manitoba, Saskatchewan, Alberta, and British Columbia.

Several Canadian model forests are located in the boreal forest: the Western Newfoundland Model Forest; the Waswanipi Cree Model Forest in northern Quebec; the Lake Abitibi Model Forest in Ontario; the Manitoba Model Forest; the Prince Albert Model Forest in Saskatchewan; and sections of the Bas-Saint-Laurent Model Forest in Quebec, of the Foothills Model Forest in Alberta, and of the McGregor

TOP A hydraulic cutting head is used to harvest trees in this spruce stand.

BOTTOM Low-impact harvesting and retention of buffer trees have become common practices in Canada's boreal forest.

Gros Morne National Park in Newfoundland and Labrador.

TOP Kelly Thomson explains how Aboriginal people lived and traveled in the forested highlands of what is now Cypress Hills Interprovincial Park.

BOTTOM These frames catch falling seeds, allowing researchers to measure reproduction in boreal stands.

RIGHT Ken Prokop makes wine from wild blueberries harvested from the boreal forest near Weyakwin, Saskatchewan.

Model Forest in central British Columbia. Each is dedicated to developing and sharing sustainable forest management techniques at a community level.

As the twenty-first century begins, Canada's boreal forest is recognized and valued for its contribution to the economic welfare of Canadians and for its importance as part of the largest forest ecosystem on earth. The protection, preservation, conservation, and ongoing sustainable management of the boreal forest demonstrate Canada's commitment to its stewardship.

Canadian Forest Service researcher Susan Cassidy checks an insect trap for beetles as part of a biodiversity study in northwestern Alberta.

GREAT LAKES–ST. LAWRENCE
FOREST

The autumnal beauty of this forest makes it one of Canada's most visited and well-known natural areas

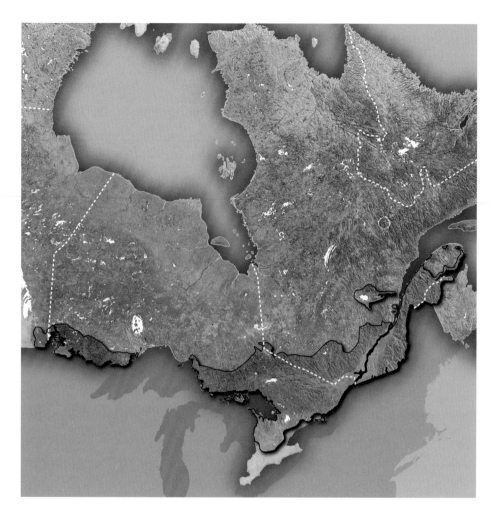

Across a broad section of south-central and eastern Canada stretch forests characterized by their mixture of broadleaf and coniferous trees. The Great Lakes–St. Lawrence forest covers 273 690 km², or about 6.6% of the total forest area of Canada. It begins in southern Manitoba, where its most western limit occurs just south of Lake Winnipeg. The forest extends eastward through Canada in a broad band north of the Rainy River, Lake Superior, Lake Huron, Georgian Bay, and eastern Lake Ontario. In Quebec, it follows the north shore of the St. Lawrence River as far east as Québec City and its south shore to the eastern extremity of the Gaspé peninsula, where it touches the Atlantic Ocean.

North of Lake Superior between Thunder Bay and Wawa, Ontario, the Great Lakes–St. Lawrence forest is broken by a 300-km section of boreal forest. In southwestern Ontario, along the north shore of Lake Erie and western Lake Ontario, the Great Lakes–St. Lawrence forest borders the Carolinian forest. A small isolated section, 175 km north of its continuous range, encircles Lac Saint-Jean in south-central Quebec.

Most stands in the Great Lakes–St. Lawrence forest include a strong component of broadleaf and coniferous species, as well as a rich shrub and herbaceous understory. The forest is often described as transitional, intermediate between the mainly coniferous boreal forest to the north and the Carolinian forest to the south. However, in its particular associations of coniferous and broadleaf trees, a forest of clearly recognizable character results, suggesting more than a simple overlay of two differing forest types.

Most of the forest lies in an area with gentle topography and a relatively warm summer climate. In the most northern portions, the terrain is rugged and rolling, featuring ancient Precambrian rock outcrops and shallow soils. To the west of Lake of the Woods, in southern Manitoba, the landscape becomes flat, poorly drained, and swampy. Here, the forest thins and merges with the boreal forest and prairies to the west. The most eastern extremities of the forest, along the Gaspé peninsula, receive the moderating influence of the Atlantic Ocean, resulting in a gradual transition to Acadian forest, just to the south, in northern New Brunswick.

Mixed coniferous and broadleaf stand east of Lake Superior.

TOP Lakeside camping in the forest.

BOTTOM First ice of autumn, Gatineau Park, Quebec.

RIGHT Along the Spruce Bog Trail, Algonquin Provincial Park, Ontario.

By Canadian standards, the climate of the forest is moderate. To the west of the Great Lakes, summers are warm (15°C), winters are cold (−13°C), and the mean annual precipitation is 500–700 mm. East of Lake Superior, warm summers (15°C) and rather cold winters (−9°C) are the norm; the mean annual precipitation is 800–1000 mm, exceeding 1000 mm along the Lake Superior shore. In its central portions, summers are warm (a mean of 16.5°C), winters are mild (a mean of −7°C) but snowy, and mean annual precipitation ranges between 800 and 1000 mm. At the eastern extremities of the forest, the mean summer temperature is moderate (14.5°C), the mean winter temperature relatively mild (−8°C), and the mean annual precipitation is 900–1300 mm.

Common broadleaf species in the Great Lakes–St. Lawrence forest include sugar maple, red maple, yellow birch, basswood, American beech, red oak, red ash, white ash, largetooth aspen, and ironwood. The spectacular shades of orange, yellow, and red of the eastern Canadian autumn, famous worldwide, are produced largely by these species.

Palmer Rapids on the Madawaska River, Ontario.

The characteristic conifer of the forest is eastern white pine, an historically important tree in Canada. Typically, eastern white pine and other characteristic conifers, such as red pine, eastern hemlock, and eastern white-cedar, occur in various combinations with the common broadleaf species. Smaller understory tree species include Canada plum, sweet viburnum, and alternate-leaf dogwood, all widespread in distribution. Pitch pine, a coniferous species with an extremely limited distribution in Canada, occurs in a few locations at the eastern end of Lake Ontario and farther eastward along the St. Lawrence River.

Several trees typical of the boreal forest also extend into or are distributed throughout the forest. Species such as tamarack, jack pine, white spruce, white birch, Bebb willow, and trembling aspen range southward into the forest. Eastern red-cedar, butternut, bitternut hickory, white oak, and black cherry, characteristic of the Carolinian forest to the south, also make their way here. Red spruce, a conifer more typical of the Acadian forest to the east, has a disjunct population in the eastern portion of the Great Lakes–St. Lawrence forest, 200 km from its continuous range.

A wide selection of herbaceous plants and shrubs is found beneath the forest canopy—plants such as red trillium, snow trillium, Canada mayflower, false Solomon's-seal, wild leek, Virginia strawberry, ram's head lady's slipper, dogtooth violet, and common yellow-oxalis; and shrubs such as sweet fern, eastern leatherwood, beaked hazel, trailing arbutus, common winterberry, and smooth blackberry.

The mixed broadleaf and conifer stands of the forest support a variety of animals. Common mammals are red fox, white-tailed deer, snowshoe hare, North American porcupine, and American black bear. Characteristic birds include the barred owl, black-capped chickadee, pileated woodpecker, ruffed grouse, northern goshawk, and red-shouldered hawk. A host of reptile and amphibian species occur here, including the eastern ribbon snake, northern water snake, spotted turtle, mudpuppy, red-backed salamander, Blanding's turtle, wood frog, and bullfrog.

Wildfire and windstorms are the chief natural disturbances in the Great Lakes–St. Lawrence forest, and two of the sources of its mixed character. Though now largely controlled by human intervention, wildfires historically occurred at varying scales, the largest creating extensive forests of jack pine, black spruce, red pine, and white birch. Where disturbance occurred on a smaller scale, persistent red pine and eastern white pine forests often developed. Localized disturbance resulted in small-scale gaps in which shade-tolerant species such as eastern hemlock, red spruce, eastern white-cedar, and balsam fir became established, often mixing with smaller understory broadleaf trees.

The Great Lakes–St. Lawrence forest has long been home to Aboriginal peoples. The extensive network of lakes and rivers throughout the area provided rapid transportation and ready access to hunting and gathering grounds. Evidence of culturally and spiritually important Aboriginal sites, including burial grounds, pictographs, agricultural areas, traditional camps, and portages, can be found throughout the forest.

Under the Canadian constitution, provincial governments oversee publicly owned forest resources within their boundaries. Each province develops and administers its own legislation and policies regarding forests. The provinces determine allowable harvest levels, allocate timber licenses, and collect cutting fees from harvesting activities on crown land.

The federal government's responsibility for forestry lies in international trade and relations, consensus building among stakeholders, Aboriginal affairs, and the national reporting of statistics. The national body in Canada that provides leadership in forest matters is the Canadian Council of Forest Ministers, composed of forest ministers from each of the 10 provinces and 3 territories, along with their federal counterpart.

European colonization of eastern Canada resulted in extensive modification of the ecosystems of the area. In the late 1700s, sizable areas of the forest were felled, burned, and turned over to agricultural use. Thereafter, exploitation of timber resources became an organized enterprise, and timber rapidly surpassed agricultural products and fur as the most important export resource in Canada. The history of the Great Lakes–St. Lawrence forest from this time onward is very much the history of Canada itself. Many of the cities and towns of eastern Canada, including Ottawa, Canada's capital, can trace their location and existence to the river drives of massive logs harvested from this area.

Throughout the nineteenth century, one-third of the revenues in crown treasuries came from the sale of eastern white pine. In Ontario alone, fees collected from the harvest of this species are estimated to have been that province's single greatest source of revenue until the early part of the twentieth century. While the great pines furnished square timbers prized for ship's masts, oaks and maples provided planks and

Canoeing the Madawaska River, Ontario.

structural materials. Eastern hemlock was extensively harvested for its bark, which provided tannin, and for its timber, which provided railway ties. After the white pine industry had exhausted available supplies to sustain that trade, successive industries developed to cut spruce, pine, and fir species as structural lumber and pulp logs for the paper-making industry.

The last two centuries have seen large parts of the Great Lakes – St. Lawrence forest altered in structure and continuity. Today's forest is more fragmented and composed of trees of smaller dimension than in pre-European times. Nonetheless, the forest remains an intrinsic element of the eastern Canadian landscape — ecologically sound, vigorous, and productive. Nearly 90% of the forest, 245 490 km^2, is classified as timber-productive.

Challenges facing contemporary forest managers are the decline in the quantity and quality of long-lived forest species, such as eastern white pine, and the ongoing conversion of stands to pioneer species, such as poplar and white birch. As a result,

much of the forest research in the Great Lakes–St. Lawrence forest focuses on the development and assessment of silvicultural practices that will ensure successful regeneration of existing white and red pine stands.

Current approaches to harvesting and regenerating the forest vary, reflecting the mixed and complex character of the forest. On sites where eastern white pine is dominant, a shelterwood harvesting system is often used. In this system, mature trees are harvested in a series of two or more cuts. The initial partial cut increases the amount of sunlight reaching the forest floor; an overhead canopy is retained, which provides shade and is a source of seeds. This system favors the regeneration of eastern white pine.

In mixed stands of shade-tolerant species, such as eastern hemlock, sugar maple, and yellow birch, a selection system is often used, where only a small portion of the forest is harvested at a given time. The majority of trees remaining on a site are retained, providing a source of seed and shade for regeneration of the stand.

LEFT A pair of mergansers, Algonquin Provincial Park, Ontario.

RIGHT Beaver lodge, Gatineau Park, Quebec.

LEFT An aspen grove indicating a disturbed site in the forest.

RIGHT Stephan Rauschenberger selection logging using horses in the Haliburton Forest and Wildlife Reserve, Haliburton, Ontario.

At the northern limits of the forest, where transition to the boreal forest occurs, extensive wildfires have left a legacy of large even-aged conifer forest stands; here jack pine, black spruce, and white birch often predominate. Because the stands are adapted to natural disturbance and unable to regenerate unless growing in full sunlight, most trees of commercial value are harvested at one time. Strategically placed trees are often left on site to act as natural seed banks, and this substantial natural regeneration is supplemented by seeding and tree planting.

A broad range of ecosystem components in the forest are subjects of scientific study, including understory plant diversity, forest succession patterns, forest insect populations, and the transfer of nutrients in forest systems. Old-growth forests, and the intricate relationships that exist among the various plant and animal communities they support, are of particular interest. The role of old-growth forests in maintaining biological diversity at local and regional scales is currently being evaluated as a potential indicator of sustainable forest management.

Unintentional introductions of alien insects such as gypsy moth and diseases such as white pine blister rust and butternut canker have significantly altered the distribution, quality, and species richness of the Great Lakes–St. Lawrence forest. Attempts to develop resistant trees and environmentally sensitive pest control methods form a large part of current forest research.

The Great Lakes–St. Lawrence forest provides a wide range of nontimber resources—fur harvesting, mushroom growing, and berry crop production to name just a few. In 2001, maple sugar production, a traditional nontimber resource in the forest, resulted in the export of about 25.9 million litres of maple syrup.

In the last 60 years, recreation in the forest has become very popular. Ecotourism and forest recreation are significant components of local economies. Tens of thousands of rugged lakes and rivers can be found here in eastern Canada's "cottage country." Research into recreational preferences in the area suggests people prefer to camp, canoe, hunt, or hike in landscapes that include eastern white pine and red pine.

TOP Piling logs after felling. Only a small portion of this forest will be harvested at a given time.

BOTTOM Tyler Peet taking a break. Small-scale harvesting operations are common in the Great Lakes–St. Lawrence forest.

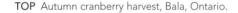

TOP Autumn cranberry harvest, Bala, Ontario.

BOTTOM Berry crop production is one of many nontimber resources of the area.

RIGHT Dr. Ben Wang selecting seeds to produce improved eastern white pines, Canadian Forest Service, Petawawa Research Forest.

The Great Lakes–St. Lawrence forest includes the Eastern Ontario Model Forest. Its 15 000 km² covers many diverse areas including Canada's National Capital Region and lands of the Mohawk community of Akwesasne. Projects in the model forest focus on monitoring the state of the forest, measuring the effectiveness of maple sap collection systems, and establishing a database for biodiversity. Demonstration sites showcase activities such as cultivation of native plants of medicinal value, effective management of sugar maple stands, and more efficient thinning of red pine plantations. Also located in the forest are sections of the 1131-km² Bas-Saint-Laurent Model Forest in eastern Quebec.

Three of Canada's national parks are found in the forest, two of them in Ontario—Georgian Bay Islands and St. Lawrence Islands. La Mauricie National Park is in Quebec. Many nature reserves, conservation areas, and provincial parks, including Birch Point Park in Manitoba, Algonquin Park in Ontario, and Gatineau Park in Quebec, are located in the forest.

Spreading root system of an eastern white pine.

The varied character, richness of species, historical context, and autumnal beauty of the Great Lakes–St. Lawrence forest make it one of the most visited and well-known natural areas in Canada. Its importance as a source of high-quality forest resources and proximity to Canada's populated south enhance its status as an ecologically and economically significant forest.

CAROLINIAN
FOREST

*The future of Canada's smallest and most southern forest
depends on the concern of Canadians*

South of Canada's vast northern forests, south even of the colorful mixed maple and conifer stands of the Great Lakes–St. Lawrence forest, is a triangular peninsula, tucked neatly between Lakes St. Clair and Huron to the northwest and Lakes Ontario and Erie to the southeast. It is the most southern part of Canada—so far south that a line drawn westward on a map from its most southern point would intersect the northern border of California. This area, atypical in a country noted for its vast northern wilderness, is Canada's Carolinian forest.

The Carolinian forest covers 550 km from east to west, occupying a total of 4310 km^2, just 0.1% of the total forest area of Canada. Northeast, it extends from Windsor and Sarnia, Ontario, along the shores of Lakes St. Clair and Huron as far as Goderich, Ontario. Eastward, it tracks the north shores of Lakes Erie and Ontario, never extending more than 70 km north from either lake's shoreline. Beyond that distance, the Carolinian forest merges into the more evenly mixed conifer and broadleaf forests of the Great Lakes–St. Lawrence forest. Just beyond Belleville and to the north

of the sand dunes of Prince Edward County, Ontario, at its most eastern point, the Carolinian forest again merges into the surrounding Great Lakes–St. Lawrence forest.

Humid, warm to hot summers and mild snowy winters characterize the area spanned by the Carolinian forest. The mean annual temperature is 9°C in the extreme southwestern portion of the area and 8°C farther north. Some evidence suggests the northern frontier of the area is associated with the 8°C isotherm, a boundary line defining that part of Ontario where the average daily temperature for the year is 8°C or greater. The mean summer temperature reaches 18°C and the mean winter temperature –2.5°C. The mean annual precipitation ranges between 750 and 900 mm. Precipitation is evenly distributed throughout the year. In summer, the meeting of warm and cold air masses coupled with convective heating and ample available moisture from the surrounding Great Lakes produces frequent heavy thunderstorms.

The name "Carolinian" refers to the many plant and animal species in the forest that have natural ranges radiating from a point far to the southeast, in the Piedmont

Tangled vines in Backus Woods near Long Point, the largest tract of old-growth Carolinian forest in Canada.

region of North Carolina. Several species occur as far south as the Gulf of Mexico, but reach the extreme northern limit of their distribution in Canada. A recognizable feature of the forest is the relatively small proportion of conifer species. The Carolinian forest is the only occurrence in Canada of the vast broadleaf forest system of the eastern United States. Uneven-aged broadleaf trees dominate forest stands, and there is generally a well-defined layer of smaller trees and shrubs beneath the dominant and subdominant tree canopy.

Although Canada's smallest forest type, the Carolinian forest contains a greater number of native tree species, more than 70, than any other of the forest types. The forest provides habitat to over 2000 plant species, 400 bird species, and 47 species of reptiles and amphibians. Significantly, the Carolinian forest also has many of the plant and animal species considered by the Committee on the Status of Endangered Wildlife in Canada to be at risk. Chiefly because of habitat loss from land use changes and urbanization, red mulberry, cucumber magnolia, American ginseng, three birds orchid, brown widelip orchid, and devil's-tongue (prickly-pear) are endangered and facing imminent extirpation in Canada. The Kentucky coffeetree is threatened and considered likely to become endangered. Blue ash and common hoptree are species of special concern because of their particular sensitivity to human activities and natural events.

The Carolinian forest shares certain characteristics with the Great Lakes– St. Lawrence forest. Both forests are largely composed of sugar maple, basswood, American beech, red maple, and red, white, and bur oak. Eastern white pine occurs in small stands on drier sites and eastern hemlock is found on cool, moist, north-facing slopes. Eastern white-cedar is present on escarpments and eastern redcedar is found on gravelly or rocky limestone sites.

However, it is the southern flora and fauna that make this forest unique. Species found here that occur naturally nowhere else in Canada include eastern flowering dogwood, wild crab apple, shellbark hickory, red hickory, pawpaw, redbud, American sycamore, burning-bush euonymus, black tupelo, sassafras, tulip-tree, black oak, pin oak, and dwarf chinquapin oak.

In a few locations in the Carolinian forest, open areas of oak savanna and tallgrass prairie occur. Rare habitats in Ontario, these sites have resulted from, and still depend on, environmental stresses such as fire, drought, and spring flooding. Many of the tallgrass species, including big bluestem, little bluestem, and sideoats grama, are of special ecological concern because of their limited distribution. Black, swamp white, white, and pin oak, species with relatively restricted distributions in Canada, are an important component of the forest's savanna areas.

Unusual forest species include poison-sumac, a tree-sized species closely related to poison-ivy, and two tree species only recently authenticated as native to Canada— Ohio buckeye, which occurs naturally only on Walpole Island at the north end of Lake St. Clair, and pumpkin ash, a little-known species that occurs in a few locations at the west end of Lake Erie.

The fauna of the forest is equally unique in Canada. For instance, the Virginia opossum (Canada's only native marsupial), the fox squirrel, and the flying squirrel

are found here. Characteristic bird species include the northern mockingbird, hooded warbler, and orchard oriole. Several migratory birds such as the Acadian flycatcher, Carolina wren, blue-gray gnatcatcher, red-bellied woodpecker, and yellow-breasted chat reach the northern portion of their range in the forest.

Reptiles and amphibians include the eastern milk snake, eastern fox snake, queen snake, eastern massasauga rattlesnake, five-lined skink, spiny softshell turtle, Jefferson salamander, Fowler's toad, and the rare northern cricket frog. Giant swallowtails, common buckeye butterflies, and about 50 species of spiders and insects that are not present elsewhere in Canada also occur here.

The Carolinian forest was the scene of some of Canada's early history. It was already the home of Aboriginal peoples when traveled by seventeenth-century French explorers. United Empire Loyalists fleeing the United States after the Revolutionary War subsequently settled the area. Much of the forest was felled and burned to make way for the fields, farms, and settlements of what would become Upper Canada.

A forested valley in the Morris Tract Provincial Nature Reserve, east of Goderich. Located at the northern limit of the Carolinian forest, the reserve shelters 14 species of plants classified as provincially rare.

The Marsh Boardwalk in Point Pelee National Park on Lake Erie.

As early as 1830 the forest supplied eastern white pine for the square timber trade, after which most of the remaining broadleaf forests were progressively harvested for their high quality lumber. Today, the Carolinian forest is primarily agricultural land, as well known for its vineyards, orchards, and productive vegetable farms as it is for its unique flora and fauna.

Although most of its old growth has been lost, about 4030 km^2, or 93.5% of the existing forest, is classified as timber-productive. Forest management efforts are not on the scale of the more northerly forests, and most harvesting involves the selection and felling of individual trees. Numerous red and Scots pine plantations were started early in the twentieth century. Extensive fruit orchards and even nut tree plantations have also been established.

The Carolinian forest is currently under severe pressure from agricultural activity and an expanding urban population. Natural forest cover and wildlife habitat have been greatly reduced. About 7.5 million people, or 25% of Canada's population, live

TOP Scattered cottonwoods on the shores of Lake Ontario, Presqu'ile Provincial Park, near Belleville.

BOTTOM Black oak savanna regenerating after a controlled burn near Turkey Point Provincial Park.

LEFT Shifting sands mark the forest edge along the western shoreline of Point Pelee National Park.

LEFT Large silver maples dominate this seasonal flood plain in Backus Woods.

RIGHT Introduced to Canada, golden weeping willow trees are now a common feature around Carolinian marshes and wetlands.

within the area. As that population grows, pressures on woodlands will increase. The Carolinian forest has been reduced to less than 10% of its original extent, and the fragmented areas remaining are encircled by agricultural activity and urban sprawl. Tallgrass and savanna oak sites have been severely affected and now cover less than 5% of their original extent.

Private woodlots and conservation areas in the forest are increasingly recognized as valuable genetic and economic resources. Outreach programs and management methods aimed at restoring old-growth forest have been developed, and private woodlot owners are encouraged to re-create conditions that existed in the forest previous to European settlement. Management guidelines for maintaining old-growth features include maintenance of forest canopy gaps, encouragement of ground cover development, and the retention of dead "snag" trees as habitat for wildlife.

Horticultural organizations, botanical gardens, and arboreta are documenting, propagating, and preserving the diverse species of the Carolinian forest. University and government research programs are working toward the recovery and reintroduction of white elm and American chestnut, species severely affected by alien fungal pathogens. Also ongoing is DNA identification of red mulberry, a species that has become rare because of hybridization with the introduced white mulberry. Only six populations remain in Canada, all in the Carolinian forest. Plant and animal populations that reach the northern limit of their distribution in the forest are a particularly important genetic resource that can indicate future climate change.

The ecological value and unique quality of the Carolinian forest is recognized by Canadians and their governments. Societies and nongovernmental organizations dedicated to the preservation, restoration, and sustainable management of the forest are numerous, and several provincial parks and conservation areas have been established. Parks include The Pinery, Rondeau, Short Hills, and Presqu'ile. Provincial nature reserves include Ojibway Prairie, Fish Point, and Trillium Woods. Point Pelee National Park is located here, at the most southern point of mainland Canada. Famous for its flora and geography, it is particularly favored by bird-watchers as a location to observe migratory birds that regularly travel through the area.

Perhaps no forest in Canada depends more on the interest and concern of its human population than the Carolinian. It will continue to exist only if its unique biological diversity is considered worth retaining and protecting against the competing pressures of population growth and alternative land-use applications. The future survival of Canada's Carolinian forest will indicate the sustainability of all forests, large and small, in Canada.

TOP An open stand of mature black oak in Rondeau Provincial Park.

BOTTOM John E. Brownlie, a park naturalist, assists bird-watchers in Point Pelee National Park; 370 species of migrating birds have been recorded here.

WESTERN
FORESTS

Subalpine forest on the upper slopes of Little Highwood Pass, Kananaskis country, Alberta.

In Canada's western provinces of British Columbia and Alberta, a series of rugged mountain systems, each composed of several ranges, profoundly affects regional climate and vegetation. Four types of forest are found here: subalpine, Columbia, montane, and coastal. Their distribution is affected by topography to a much greater extent than that of forests in eastern Canada. As a result, western forests are arranged in series of strata, beginning at sea level and in the deep river valleys and terminating at the tree line of the high mountain peaks.

From north to south, the western forests cover about 10 degrees of latitude, extending from the boreal forest in northern British Columbia to the 49th parallel in the south. Species types and associations are affected by local climatic conditions and by cold arctic air masses flowing southward down the valleys between mountain ranges. From west to east, conditions vary profoundly, ranging from maritime influences at low elevation along the coast, to continental influences at relatively high baseline elevations in the interior.

Canada's western forests contain an unusually high percentage of mature and overmature timber. The late development of forest harvesting in the west, relative to that in eastern Canada, and the effective suppression of wildfire, have resulted in forests with large trees that produce high-value forest products and many old-growth stands that increase the diversity of wildlife habitat.

Isolated by geography and composed of a wide range of ecosystem and habitat types, the western forests are the most biologically diverse in Canada. British Columbia and Alberta combined are habitat for over 50% of all species of mammals native to Canada, and the former is home to 29 mammal species found nowhere else in the country. Over 70% of resident Canadian bird species occur in British Columbia, more species than in any other Canadian province. As well, 21 amphibian species and 17 reptiles are also native to British Columbia.

The importance of retaining this biological richness has been recognized, and 13% of the overall land base in British Columbia, about 125 000 km^2, is protected land, unavailable for harvesting or other such forest-resource exploitation. Included in this total are 113 000 km^2 of provincial parks and nature reserves, including the 3211-km^2 Kitlope Heritage Conservancy, which contains the world's largest intact coastal temperate rain forest, and the 449-km^2 Khutzeymateen Grizzly Bear Sanctuary, the only grizzly bear sanctuary in Canada.

The western forests are also extremely productive. About 250 000 km^2, or 42%, of British Columbia's forests is classified as commercial and available for harvesting; they account for about 85% of the plywood produced in Canada and almost half of Canada's softwood lumber exports. Yet only about 1900 km^2 is harvested annually.

Much of the research in the western forests focuses on analyzing landscape composition, developing land-use decision-making tools, and determining the impact of forest management approaches on biodiversity and other forest values. Currently, the protection of forest stands from insect pests, particularly the mountain pine beetle, and from pathogens and parasites such as armillaria root disease and dwarf mistletoe, is of great concern.

Researchers are also working to better understand forest growth, yield, and regeneration responses, nutrient cycles, and dynamics. Developing methods to measure forest processes and monitor change in forest biodiversity is of particular interest, as these methods can be directly applied to creating effective, ecologically based forest management and silvicultural systems. Socioeconomic aspects of forest management, Aboriginal traditional knowledge, and nontimber forest products are recent and growing areas of forest research.

Western Canada's geographic isolation, mountainous terrain, particular climatic conditions, and short history of resource exploitation have produced forests diverse in landscape, species, and timber types. This may partially explain why these forests generate such profound interest, reverence, and passion in Canada and around the world.

TOP Lodgepole pine in the Columbia forest near Weigert Creek, British Columbia.

BOTTOM Rocky Mountain Douglas-fir in the montane forest near Osoyoos, British Columbia.

SUBALPINE
FOREST

The subalpine forest is a unique combination of productive stands and scattered diminutive trees

PRECEDING PAGES Subalpine forest south of Top of the World Provincial Park , British Columbia.

BELOW At the tree line, subalpine forest is replaced by alpine meadows, glaciers, and snowfields.

The subalpine forest is found on the mountain slopes of British Columbia and western Alberta; its coniferous stands are specifically adapted to the rigors of a high-altitude environment. The subalpine forest covers 165 690 km², or 4.0% of the total forest area of Canada. It begins at elevations where the coastal, montane, and Columbia forests end and extends to the tree line, where it is replaced by alpine meadows, glaciers, and snowfields. Diverse and biologically rich, it varies from abundant, highly productive closed-canopy stands, where Engelmann spruce grow 15 m tall in 50 years, to scattered diminutive stands near the tree line, where the oldest trees are no more than a few metres high after a hundred years.

Climate varies widely in the subalpine forest. Typically, summers are cool and prone to early frosts, while winters are long and cold. Mean summer temperatures reach about 12°C in many parts of the area, and mean winter temperatures are around −6.5° to −11°C. In parts of the forest, snow covers the ground for eight months of the year.

Forest succession is driven by several factors. Wildfire, particularly on the drier, rockier sites favored by lodgepole pine, was the overriding influence until the implementation of effective wildfire suppression during the past 50–60 years. This has allowed much of the old forest to be harvested, and reforestation has become the major means of stand replacement. Natural disturbance factors, including bark beetles, root diseases, severe storms, high winds, avalanches, and landslides, also contribute to the regeneration process in the subalpine forest.

The subalpine forest separates into two types: one that grows along the Pacific coast and the other in interior British Columbia and Alberta. Along the Pacific coast, the subalpine forest is composed of yellow-cedar, mountain hemlock, western hemlock, amabilis fir, and subalpine fir. No spruce species occurs here. Isolated pockets of the subalpine forest occur atop the central mountain range of Vancouver Island, surrounded on the lower slopes by the coastal forest. The subalpine forest of the highlands of the Queen Charlotte Islands has a similar species composition, but without the fir species.

TOP Lodgepole pine and Engelmann spruce are common in the subalpine forest.

BOTTOM Forest meets alpine meadow along this trail in the Highwood Pass, Alberta.

RIGHT A carpet of mosses, shrubs, and herbaceous species covers the forest floor on moist sites.

On the interior mountain ranges of British Columbia and Alberta, the subalpine forest is dominated by Engelmann spruce, subalpine fir, and lodgepole pine. At lower altitudes in this area, these species are abundant, forming a luxuriant closed-canopy forest. White spruce and hybrids of white and Engelmann spruce are also commonly present, but white spruce gradually disappears as elevation increases. On drier interior sites at middle elevations, extensive lodgepole pine forests, produced by past wildfires, are typical. Rocky Mountain Douglas-fir and Rocky Mountain juniper are minor components of the forest mix.

At higher altitudes in the interior, subalpine fir becomes the dominant tree; whitebark pine occurs throughout most of the area on rocky ridges and along exposed slopes near the tree line. Limber pine and subalpine larch favor similar sites and elevations, but are limited in range to southern sections of the Rocky Mountains in British Columbia and Alberta. Above the tree line, heather, Hooker's mountain avens, and colorful herbs such as spreading phlox and tufted alpine saxifrage form alpine meadows.

West of the Rocky Mountains in interior British Columbia, the subalpine forest is fragmented. It occupies uplands and is surrounded at lower altitudes and in intervening valleys by montane, coastal, or Columbia forests. In southeastern British Columbia, the lower limit of the subalpine forest overlaps and merges with the Columbia forest. East of the Rocky Mountains, through the foothills of western Alberta, the subalpine forest merges into the boreal forest. White spruce mixes with, then replaces, Engelmann spruce, and lodgepole pine is common on extensive burnt-over sites. South of Calgary, Alberta, the subalpine forest borders aspen parkland and prairie grassland.

About 147 940 km^2, or 89.3%, of the subalpine forest is classified as timber-productive. In volume of wood per square kilometre on stocked, timber-productive sites, the subalpine forest is second in Canada only to the coastal forest.

Shrub and herbaceous species associated with the subalpine forest include Douglas maple, western snowberry, russet buffaloberry, common juniper, rusty menziesia, thinleaf huckleberry, heartleaf arnica, Canadian bunchberry, and twinflower. On relatively moist sites, the forest floor is often covered by a highly varied moss and lichen layer that includes species such as splendid feather moss, dicranum moss, and green dog lichen.

Common mammals of the subalpine forest include grizzly bear, moose, coyote, Canada lynx, hoary marmot, mule deer, and mountain goat. Red-tailed hawk, mountain chickadee, and red crossbill are among the bird species found, and there are a few amphibians in the area, some at relatively high altitudes, for example, the spotted frog, red-legged frog, and tailed frog.

Research in the subalpine forest focuses on the response of high-elevation forest ecosystems to a range of harvesting techniques and site-preparation treatments. Additional studies concentrate on the landscape-level integration of management for timber and nontimber resource values, including recreation, tourism, watersheds, wildlife habitat, and scenic views. This research guides forest managers in planning alternative methods of management in this unique forest type.

Canada's forests and the products they provide to the world are a major part of the Canadian economy. In 2002, forest-related activities accounted for almost 361 000 jobs. More than 300 communities across Canada list forestry as their primary source of employment. Canada's forests also produce substantial nonconsumptive economic benefits, supporting a recreation and tourism industry that generates expenditures of several billion dollars for outdoor activities in natural areas such as wildlife viewing, recreational fishing, and hunting.

Sections of the 27 500-km² Foothills Model Forest, including parts of Jasper National Park, lie within the subalpine forest. The model forest involves more than 60 partners representing a variety of industries, academia, government, and local communities. Research in the model forest focuses on the impact of forest use on the local environment and economy and on the identification of methods by which the ecological, social, and economic sustainability of the forest can be measured.

Canada's subalpine forest landscapes are world famous. The discovery, in 1883, of the Cave and Basin Hot Springs at Banff, Alberta, led to the establishment of Canada's oldest and probably most famous national park, Banff National Park. Lake Louise and Jasper National Park in Alberta also attract a flood of visitors from around the world. As ski lifts and gondolas ascend the mountains, they offer visitors a spectacular view of the forest's changing composition.

Besides Banff and Jasper, several national parks in British Columbia include sections of the subalpine forest: Kootenay, Yoho, and Mount Revelstoke. Provincial

TOP These hikers near Golden, British Columbia, are participating in a race testing their physical endurance.

BOTTOM Mule deer occupy steep terrains and open conifer forests.

RIGHT Mount Robson Provincial Park, part of the Canadian Rocky Mountains Parks World Heritage Site, is in one of the world's largest protected areas.

parks in the subalpine forest include Willmore Wilderness Park in Alberta and Strathcona and Kakwa provincial parks in British Columbia.

Diverse and intriguing, the subalpine forest presents a unique combination of highly productive forest stands, highly specialized tree species, spectacular landscape, wildlife habitat, and unparalleled outdoor recreation opportunities.

A mountain waterfall in the rugged terrain west of Glacier National Park, British Columbia.

COLUMBIA
FOREST

Although not extensive, this lush, interior forest is both productive and richly diverse

PRECEDING PAGES Columbia forest surrounding Lake Revelstoke, southwestern British Columbia.

BELOW Ample moisture in the Columbia forest
promotes lush growth similar to that of the coastal
forest.

A forest similar to the lush, productive coastal forest is found in southeastern British Columbia. The Columbia forest covers 39 080 km^2, about 0.9% of the total forest area of Canada. It owes its lushness and diversity to eastward moving air masses that shed moisture as they are forced upward over inland mountain chains.

Long, warm summers are common in the Columbia forest, and the snowpack at alpine elevations provides additional moisture during the warm season. Winters are cool and wet. The mean summer temperature for the area is 14°C and the mean winter temperature −5°C. Mean annual precipitation can range up to 1200 mm, but to the west, at the borders of the forest, the climate becomes drier, and precipitation declines to 500–800 mm annually.

The abundant growth of the Columbia forest begins in the deep valley trenches and continues to about 1200 m, where it is replaced by subalpine forest. To the west and south, where precipitation and plant growth are more restricted, along the lower slopes and valleys below about 750 m, it gives way to dry montane forest or grassland.

At its northern boundary, subalpine fir, as well as white spruce, Engelmann spruce, and their intermediate hybrid forms increase in frequency. On dry sites, particularly where wildfire has occurred, extensive stands of Rocky Mountain Douglas-fir are found. Along riverbanks and areas where flowing water deposits silts and gravels, black cottonwood mixes with western redcedar and Engelmann spruce. On wet sites along the upper Fraser Valley, scattered stands of black spruce occur with white spruce.

The wetter parts of the Columbia forest are often referred to as an interior wetbelt or as temperate inland rain forest. Certainly many of the tree species adapted to the moist and humid conditions of the coastal forest occur here. Western redcedar and western hemlock dominate older stands, but on drier sites may grow in association with Rocky Mountain Douglas-fir or ponderosa pine. Grand fir is often present, and white birch is frequently found in gaps created by root disease. Black cottonwood commonly grows on valley bottoms and alluvial flood plains. Small trees, such as bitter cherry, western yew, cascara buckthorn, serviceberry, hawthorn, Douglas

Devil's-club, a coarse shrub adapted to moist soils and stream-side sites, is widespread in the Columbia forest.

Black cottonwood in the Elk River valley, near Hosmer.

TOP Western redcedar, Engelmann spruce, and subalpine fir in a northern section of the Columbia forest near Bounding Creek.

BOTTOM Old-growth Rocky Mountain Douglas-fir near Killam Creek.

RIGHT An old forest road near Rossland.

maple, and blue-berry elder, species common to the coastal forest, can also be found in the Columbia forest.

The Columbia forest differs from the coastal forest in several ways. Western larch, for example, common on disturbed sites in the southern Columbia forest, is absent in the coastal forest. A greater proportion of the Columbia forest is disturbed by fire, wind, insects, and avalanche. In the past, occasional summer droughts and lightning storms resulted in moderate intensity fires that have created gaps in the forest interspersed with stands differing in age and in species composition. Today, fire is usually suppressed and is not as significant a factor in forest succession.

Typical plants and shrubs in the rich understory of the Columbia forest include Canadian bunchberry, black huckleberry, thimbleberry, grouse whortleberry, heartleaf foamflower, Canada lily, northern bedstraw, many lichen and moss species, devil's-club, Oregon boxleaf, oval-leaf blueberry, western oak fern, and bride's-bonnet. Cascade azalea, black huckleberry, and fireweed are common on mid-elevation burnt-over sites.

Mule deer, Columbian ground squirrel, grizzly bear, American black bear, woodland caribou, mountain goat, and waptiti (or elk) are some of the mammals found in the forest. Chestnut-backed chickadee, American pipit, gray jay, golden-crowned sparrow, Steller's jay, ruffed grouse, white-tailed ptarmigan, and pileated woodpecker are a few of the forest's many bird species. Amphibians and reptiles include the western painted turtle, western toad, Columbia spotted frog, long-toed salamander, northern alligator lizard, rubber boa, and western terrestrial garter snake.

The Columbia forest's mix of old stands of high-volume large trees and carefully managed second-growth stands are an important part of the British Columbia forest industry. About 36 190 km², or 92.6%, of the forest is classified as timber-productive. Because of its high productivity and easily accessed position on lower mountain slopes, the Columbia forest has been extensively developed for timber production. As well, mining and hydroelectric power production contribute to the local economy.

Outdoor recreation in the Columbia forest is a significant resource for the regional economy. The old-growth western redcedar and western hemlock stands attract those interested in forest ecology. Hiking, hunting, and mountain climbing are popular pastimes as are fishing and boating on the many interior lakes in the forest area.

The Columbia forest is a component of several British Columbia parks: Mount Revelstoke and Glacier national parks, which both contain Columbia forest at their lowest elevations, and Gilnockie, Gladstone, and Wells Gray provincial parks.

An inland rain forest, rich in biological diversity, important as an economic resource, yet geographically restricted in extent and altitude, the Columbia forest typifies the productivity and ecological specialization of Canada's forests.

In 2001, exports of Canadian forest products resulted in a trade surplus of $34 billion, accounting for 58% of Canada's $59.4 billion total trade surplus. Every province and territory of Canada had a trade surplus in forest products.

Canada is the largest exporter of forest products; in 2001, 18.4% of the world's forest products exports were Canadian.

In terms of production, Canada supplies 21.7% of the world's newsprint, 14.9% of its wood pulp, and 17.2% of its softwood lumber.

MONTANE
FOREST

A forest parkland east of the Coast Mountains, the montane forest is complex, varied, rugged, and fragile

PRECEDING PAGES Wind and water erosion created these hoodoos in the montane forest near Fairmont Hot Springs, British Columbia.

BELOW Because of reduced occurrence of wildfire, lodgepole pine has become the most common tree species in the montane forest.

In the mountainous terrain of central British Columbia are complex and varied forest stands specifically adapted to survival in the extensive, dry rain-shadow zone east of the Coast Mountains. This is the montane forest, a northern extension of the forests found on the mountainous to rolling terrain of Oregon, Washington, Idaho, and western Montana. The montane forest occupies a zone below the high-altitude subalpine forest and outside the lush interior wet-belt valleys of the adjacent Columbia forest. The montane forest is typically parkland; on the very driest rocky or sandy sites, it gives way to grassland. Recently, however, the widespread exclusion of wildfire from the area has created forest stands that are considerably more dense than the original postglacial forests.

In British Columbia, the montane forest spans much of the southern interior, extending north across the plateaus of the Fraser and Nechako Rivers. Farther east, in the rain shadow of the Selkirk and Purcell Mountains, the forest follows the Kootenay River valley. On the east slope of the Rocky Mountains in southwestern

Montane forest on the banks of the Fraser River, west of Williams Lake.

Alberta are three distinct and fragmented areas of the montane forest. The first lies along the Athabasca River, north of Jasper; another west of Calgary between Banff and Kananaskis; and a third in the area of the Porcupine Hills and Waterton Lakes. Collectively, the montane forest covers 120 750 km^2, or 2.9% of the total forest area of Canada.

Lodgepole pine has become the most common tree of the montane forest, making up about 30% of the stands in the dry southwestern interior and 60% of stands on the Nechako and Fraser Plateaus. It is progressively more widespread toward the northern boundary of the forest, where it occurs in extensive pure stands. On the southern half of the Nechako Plateau, lodgepole pine stands alternate with trembling aspen groves, which are characteristic on moister sites.

Rocky Mountain Douglas-fir (often called interior Douglas-fir) is a characteristic species throughout most of the montane forest. Its distribution extends from across the border with the United States to north of 55° latitude, at the frontier with the

subalpine forest. Stockier, smaller, and slower growing than the coastal variety, Rocky Mountain Douglas-fir is better adapted to cold and drought than its coastal counterpart. The ground cover beneath Douglas-fir stands is often exclusively pine-grass, though on the very driest sites, where stands become increasingly open and park-like, wheatgrass, junegrass, and fescues become common.

Ponderosa pine is the third characteristic species of the montane forest. It has a more southerly and restricted distribution in Canada than Rocky Mountain Douglas-fir, never extending north of 51° north latitude. In the United States, ponderosa pine is broadly distributed, but in Canada it is limited to low elevations along dry valleys. In the montane forest, this species normally grows with Douglas-fir in open-canopy stands on bunchgrass prairie.

In eastern British Columbia, where the montane forest borders the Columbia forest, wet-belt species such as western redcedar, western hemlock, and western larch are also present. At high altitudes, where the montane and subalpine forests meet, Engelmann spruce and subalpine fir occupy the transition zone between the two forest types. At its most northern extent, the montane forest merges with the sub-alpine forest. Douglas-fir maintains a scattered presence on warmer sites, but cold climate, high-altitude specialists such as subalpine fir, and Engelmann spruce, white spruce, and their hybrids, are the more common species.

On areas burned by wildfire, lodgepole pine, trembling aspen, and western white birch dominate; black cottonwood occupies lakesides and riverbanks. East of the Rocky Mountains in Alberta, Douglas-fir and lodgepole pine are common on warm, dry slopes, elsewhere supplemented by white and black spruce, and, at higher altitudes, by Engelmann spruce, subalpine fir, and whitebark pine. Limber pine occurs on rocky outcrops and stony soils at lower elevations.

The topography and geography of the montane forest combine to produce a highly variable climate. In the major valleys of the southwest, the mean summer temperature is about 15°C and the mean winter temperature −3.5°C, with a mean annual precipitation range of as little as 250–300 mm. Farther north on the major plateaus, precipitation increases, ranging around 400–600 mm. Toward the northwestern limits of the montane forest, along the interior foothills of the Coast Mountains of central British Columbia, the mean summer temperature is about 12.5°C and the mean winter temperature −7°C, with precipitation at higher elevations increasing to 600 mm. Winters are often severe, and snow may cover the ground for as long as five months.

Fire has played a critical role in shaping and controlling the montane forest. Under natural conditions, the frequency and intensity of wildfire occurrence determines the type and age of forests and maintains a balance between treeless savanna and parkland. On the driest sites, where ponderosa pine is prevalent, small fires occur on the forest floor as often as every 15–25 years. Similarly, Douglas-fir sites experience low-intensity fires that cover less than half a square kilometre on average every 10–20 years. Both species have adapted to this cycle by developing a thick, fire-resistant bark that allows mature trees to survive limited intensity ground fires. The regular

Fire burns on average 32 000 km² of Canadian forest each year; other disturbances, chiefly insects and diseases, affect 60 000 km². Together these disturbances annually affect about 1.6% of Canada's forest. In any given year, about 10 000 km² of Canada's forest, or 0.24% of the total, is harvested.

cycle of ground fires consumes younger trees, shrubs, and grasses, maintaining the parkland character of the montane forest.

High-intensity fires are estimated to occur every 150–250 years. They consume the crowns of mature trees as well as the grass layer below, thereby killing all trees, old and young alike, in the understory. Forest stands that develop following large-scale wildfires are often composed exclusively of lodgepole pine, a species whose seed germinates well in burnt-over areas.

As lodgepole pine stands mature, they become attractive to mountain pine beetles and are often infested and killed. The accumulation of dead trees predisposes such stands to fire, and a continuous cycle of stand destruction by fire followed by regeneration and infestation of lodgepole pine often occurs. In the wake of serious mountain pine beetle outbreaks, extensive salvage harvesting is done. As a result, in some areas, logging, not wildfire, is the major disturbance responsible for creating new lodgepole stands.

Montane, subalpine, and coastal forests meet at Duffey Lake, near Lillooet, and elements of each forest type can be found.

Open parkland in the rain shadow of the Selkirk and Purcell Mountains.

Farther north, broadleaf trees and shrubs, particularly scrub willows, trembling aspen, and white birch, are also prominent postfire species. These tend to be eventually replaced by longer-lived conifer species, resulting in a patchwork of forest stands that vary in age and composition.

The wide range of site conditions, climatic regimes, and tree mixes in the montane forest supports a variety of understory shrubs and herbaceous plants. Very dry sites are colonized by prairie grasses such as bluebunch wheatgrass, mountain rough fescue, Roemer's fescue, prairie sagewort, gray rabbitbrush, and plains prickly-pear. On Douglas-fir and ponderosa pine sites, silky lupine, western gromwell, common yarrow, foothill arnica, Saskatoon-berry, common juniper, and creeping juniper are common herbs and shrubs. The forest understory of postfire lodgepole pine stands includes kinnikinnick (bearberry), russet buffaloberry, pinegrass, and lichens. In the wetter, northern sections and on flood plains, fireweed, hawkweed, water birch, red-osier dogwood, Sitka alder, squashberry viburnum, and hollyleaved barberry are typical.

Characteristic mammals of the montane forest include deer mouse, long-tailed vole, little brown bat, yellow-pine chipmunk, American pine marten, coyote, mule deer, white-tailed deer, wapiti (or elk), and bighorn sheep. Common bird species include the sage thrasher, snowy owl, gyrfalcon, white-breasted nuthatch, white-headed woodpecker, pine grosbeak, pine siskin, three-toed woodpecker, red crossbill, and wood duck. Several amphibians and reptiles are found in the forest: the Great Basin spadefoot (toad), western toad, tiger salamander, western rattlesnake, western skink, common garter snake, and western painted turtle.

Moisture limits the growth rate and production of trees throughout much of the southern British Columbia interior. However, 117 510 km^2, or 97.3% of the montane forest, is classified as timber-productive. Harvesting and managing the forest are important parts of local and provincial economies.

In the southern portion of the montane forest, low precipitation greatly limits the growth and productivity of forest stands, and cattle grazing is the dominant land use. In the Okanagan Valley, irrigation has allowed the establishment of extensive vineyards and orchards. The southern Okanagan and lower Similkameen Valleys contain unique habitats dominated by grasses, sagebrush, antelope bitterbrush, and drought-tolerant shrubs. These ecosystems are considered endangered in Canada. Vulnerable and endangered wildlife species found here include the western rattlesnake, American badger, and burrowing owl. The area's specialized ecology also supports numerous invertebrate species that occur nowhere else in Canada.

Scientific research in the montane forest currently focuses on determining the ecosystem changes that have resulted from previous forest management practices. As well, the development of management methods that can reduce the risk and occurrence of mountain pine beetle outbreaks is of particular interest.

The montane forest includes much of the 77 000-km^2 McGregor Model Forest. The main objective of this model forest is to increase development and adoption of innovative sustainable forest management systems, both within and beyond its boundaries. The McGregor Model Forest has a diverse list of partners including municipal and provincial governments, First Nations, and industrial representatives.

The rolling landscape of the montane forest makes it a popular place for hiking, horseback riding, mountain biking, all-terrain vehicle use, cross-country skiing, and snowmobiling. Growing numbers of tourists are attracted to the forest's rivers and lakes to fish, swim, and boat. Portions of Kootenay and Waterton Lakes national parks lie in the montane forest, and it encompasses several provincial parks including Tweedsmuir, E.C. Manning, Chasm, Pinnacles, and Stuart River.

Viewed from north to south, perhaps no forest type in Canada presents so varied a range of forest landscapes and localized environments as the montane forest. The parkland, dry grass and sage meadows, mountain slopes, and broad plateaus of the montane provide a contrast between fragility and natural ruggedness that is fascinating and ecologically unique.

TOP Trembling aspen and Douglas maple add autumn color to the montane landscape.

BOTTOM Marshland west of the Kootenay River at a transition to the Columbia forest.

TOP Bighorn sheep at a habitat-enhancement project near Radium Hot Springs.

BOTTOM Western painted turtles are found in the marshes and wetlands of the southern montane forest.

RIGHT A lone Rocky Mountain Douglas-fir marks the change from montane forest to grassland.

In northern sections of the montane forest, trembling aspen becomes a prominent postfire species.

COASTAL
FOREST

*Monumental and extensive, to many around the world
the coastal forest is the embodiment of Canada*

Along Canada's Pacific coast, a temperate rain forest frames the beaches, inlets, rivers, and lower mountain slopes of British Columbia. It is a part of an extensive zone of temperate rain forest extending the length of the west coast of North America, from Kodiak Island in Alaska, southward through British Columbia and the Pacific Northwest, to the redwood forests of California.

Canada's coastal forest occupies about 74 470 km², or 1.8% of the total forest area of the country, extending from the southern border with the United States north to the Alsek River, just below 60% north latitude. Although mostly confined to a narrow band within 50 km of the Pacific Ocean, the coastal forest reaches considerably farther inland where it follows major ocean inlets and valleys of major rivers such as the Nass and Fraser. In addition to the coastal mainland of British Columbia, the Queen Charlotte Islands (known also by the Haida name, Haida Gwaii, "islands of the people") and Vancouver Island are also covered in coastal forest, except on inland mountain ranges, which, above about 900 m, support subalpine forest.

Throughout much of the coastal forest, mild temperatures, abundant rainfall, and constant high humidity have allowed trees to develop largely unimpeded by stress from climate or drought. Many tree species grow to immense proportions, some regularly reaching 60 or 70 m high. The tallest standing tree in Canada, a Sitka spruce known as the Carmanah Giant, grows in the coastal forest. It is estimated to measure 95.8 m high. Although the largest temperate rain forest in the world, the coastal forest is also highly diverse. In some portions, plant growth is actually hindered by too much rain and a lack of sunlight on the forest floor. On the other hand, the Gulf Islands, between Vancouver Island and the mainland, include dry areas that support the growth of native cacti.

The coastal forest enjoys one of the mildest and wettest climates in Canada. The mild temperatures result from the proximity to the Pacific Ocean. The area's abundant rainfall comes from moist air masses. These move east and inland from the ocean and are forced upward by coastal mountain ranges. The water vapor in the air masses cools

Because of the abundant rainfall and humidity, trees are often lushly draped with lichens and mosses.

and condenses as it reaches higher altitudes, falling as rain or snow along the coast and the western mountain slopes.

On the British Columbia mainland and Vancouver Island, mean annual precipitation ranges from 1500 mm at the lower elevations to 3500 mm at higher ones. As befits a maritime climate, there is relatively little variation throughout the year in mean monthly temperatures, with summer and winter means of 13.5°C and −1°C, respectively, on the British Columbia mainland, and 13.5°C and 3.5°C on west Vancouver Island. In a few isolated locations, notably the Strait of Georgia between the lower British Columbia mainland and Vancouver Island, mean annual precipitation declines to 600 mm. Farther north, mean winter temperatures decline somewhat, to about −4.5°C, and mean annual precipitation is 2000 mm along the coast and 1500 mm farther inland.

The coastal forest is dominated by a small number of coniferous species. The broadleaf trees present are mostly pioneers that occur early in the ecological succession of the forest. Although their presence in the forest canopy is limited, broadleaf species are well represented in a thick and varied shrub and small tree layer that is often present below the dominant conifers. Wind storms, diseases, and insects are common disturbances. Occurring irregularly over small areas, their actions produce a patchwork forest landscape containing trees of varying ages. The forest floor, kept constantly moist, over long periods of time accumulates a thick layer of humus and decaying plant material. Surprisingly, fire plays an important part in this forest's ecology. Douglas-fir commonly regenerates after forest fires, logging, or other disturbances. As they age, Douglas-firs develop bark layers up to 30 cm thick, making them resistant to small-scale fires. Because the area's prevailing wet climate limits the occurrence of large-scale fires, Douglas-fir and the more shade-tolerant western redcedar and grand fir are often able to attain advanced ages, regularly exceeding 400 years.

In the southern portion of the forest, the characteristic species are western hemlock, western redcedar, and coast Douglas-fir. At low elevations on the British Columbia mainland, grand fir is a common species, and along riverbanks and rich flood plains, large Sitka spruce and black cottonwood are frequently found. Western white pine is also present, though its numbers have been greatly reduced by white pine blister rust. Bigleaf maple and red alder are among the most common broadleaf species. The landscape of coastal bogs and wetlands features small, twisted shore pine. At higher elevations on mountain slopes, yellow-cedar and mountain hemlock become increasingly common in the transition to subalpine forest.

The coast of British Columbia, opposite northern Vancouver Island, features a broad rolling belt of lowland swamps and cedar bogs. Farther north, the terrain is characterized by U-shaped glaciated valleys situated at the ends of deep and rugged inlets. Douglas-fir is less abundant than it is farther south. Common species are western hemlock and amabilis fir on drier sites and western redcedar on wet sites. Along riverbanks, Sitka spruce and western redcedar grow with black cottonwood and bigleaf maple.

Depending on definition, between 7% and 19% of Canada's contemporary forest can be classified as old-aged, or old-growth, forest. The definition varies according to forest type, to the individual life span of tree species, and to the frequency of a disturbance such as fire that limits the life span of trees. For instance, if tree age and forest type are used as a basis, 18% of Canada's forests can be considered old growth. If forest land that has never been harvested is included, then 70% of Canada's forests qualify as old growth.

Inland, and at higher elevations, the coastal forest gives way to the subalpine forest, and hybridization between Sitka spruce and Engelmann spruce occurs. Northward, characteristic subalpine species are found at progressively lower elevations, with yellow-cedar and mountain hemlock eventually occurring at sea level. At its northern extremity, the coastal forest blends into the boreal forest.

The coastal forest contains an impressive number of smaller trees including western yew, Douglas maple, red and Sitka alder, blue-berry elder, western flowering dogwood, Pacific willow, and bitter cherry. Common shrubs include poison-oak, kinnikinnick (bearberry), American twinflower, rose spirea, salmonberry, red huckleberry, devil's-club, and copperbush. Common flowers and herbs found in the forest understory are miner's lettuce, Pacific trillium, Indian-pipe, Menzie's pipsissewa, and British Columbia wild-ginger.

The Queen Charlotte Islands are situated 100 km off the coast of British Columbia. This isolation and the fact that they remained free of ice during the most

Garry oak (left) and arbutus (right) thrive in the rain shadow along southeastern Vancouver Island.

recent glacial period have resulted in associations of forest tree species that differ from those of the mainland. Coast Douglas-fir, amabilis fir, grand fir, bigleaf maple, and Douglas maple, all of which occur in the coastal forest on the mainland, are not present. On parts of the islands that have a typically humid maritime climate, western hemlock, Sitka spruce, and western redcedar are characteristic species. At elevations above about 500 m in the mountainous interior, mountain hemlock and yellow-cedar become common, forming a localized forest similar to that found on the mountains of interior Vancouver Island. Shore pine grows on sandy and rocky sites, as well as in peat bogs and along subalpine ridges. Along the windswept west coast of the Queen Charlotte Islands, stunted forests of western redcedar, yellow-cedar, and western hemlock hug the shore, interspersed with peat bogs and scattered stands of crooked, flat-topped shore pines.

The area along the southeast coast of Vancouver Island, on islands in the Strait of Georgia, and on the adjacent mainland shoreline has a climate often compared to that

of the Mediterranean—warm sunny summers and mild, wet winters. Located in a rain shadow created by Vancouver Island, its summers are long and considerably drier than those elsewhere in the coastal forest. Douglas-fir, a species adapted to surviving fire, is the area's dominant tree. Although fire is now controlled in the area, many large old Douglas-firs bear scars, suggesting that in the recent past, wildfire was a frequent occurrence. Two tree species that occur nowhere else in Canada are found here. One, Garry oak, is limited to a narrow coastal strip on Vancouver Island where it occurs on rocky outcrops and on a few scattered locations on the mainland along the Fraser River. The other, arbutus, is Canada's only native broadleaf evergreen tree. Although its range extends southward along the Pacific coast into Mexico, in Canada, it is restricted to rocky shores and forest edges around Vancouver Island and the adjacent mainland, where it rapidly colonizes sites that have been disturbed by land clearing or by fire.

The coastal forest supports a wide range of animal life. Amphibian species are many and include the rough-skinned newt, Pacific giant salamander, clouded

LEFT Red alder on a coastal wetland.

RIGHT Yellow skunk cabbage, a common plant in coastal bogs and lowlands.

Sproat Lake, inland on Vancouver Island.

TOP Killer whales are often seen where coastal forest meets sea.

BOTTOM Meares Island in Clayoquot Sound.

RIGHT Soaring 700 m above the forest floor, Stawamus Chief Mountain, near Squamish, is the world's second largest granite monolith.

salamander, tailed frog, and Pacific chorus frog. Reptiles such as the western painted turtle, northwestern garter snake, western terrestrial garter snake, and sharp-tailed snake are found in the coastal forest area. Common mammals include mule deer, American black bear, grizzly bear, wapiti (or elk), gray wolf, sea and river otter, and raccoon. Typical bird species of the coastal forest are black oystercatcher, California and mountain quail, tufted puffin, chestnut-backed chickadee, northern pygmy-owl, Steller's jay, northwestern crow, bald eagle, and Pacific loon. Several species of fish, including chinook, coho, pink, chum, and sockeye salmon, that use coastal streams and rivers to spawn and reproduce, are intricately linked to the coastal forest.

Humans too have created an intimate relationship with the coastal forest. Aboriginal peoples have for thousands of years lived in and depended on the coastal forest for shelter, tools, materials, food, and medicinal plants. With the coming of Europeans, attention focused on the economic value of the coastal forest's timber. The scale, wood quality, and accessibility of western redcedar and Douglas-fir made British Columbia a global leader in the supply of forest products to the world. Initially, common practice was to locate large trees growing along shorelines and fell them directly into the ocean, enabling easy transport of the logs to manufacturing sites. Later, railways, roads, mechanized machinery, and specialized harvesting equipment, including elevated cable systems, allowed access to forest stands farther inland, at higher elevations, and on steeper slopes.

The coastal forest today remains the most productive in Canada and annual growth rates of 1600–2000 m³ per square kilometre are easily obtainable. Overall, about 10 960 km², or 14.7% of the coastal forest, is classified as timber-productive. Forest harvesting is a critical part of the regional economy, providing employment for residents and revenue for public works and institutions. Forest practices have evolved, however, to encompass a far greater range of nontimber values and considerations. Throughout British Columbia, land-use planning is increasingly ecosystem-based, and the needs of all forest users are included in the process of forest management. In particular, fishing, hiking, kayaking, rock climbing, wildlife viewing, and other forest recreation activities are recognized as economically and socially important uses of the forest, to be protected and included when forest harvesting is considered. Similarly, the sacred sites and areas of traditional activities of Aboriginal peoples are protected.

To accommodate this wide range of values, new and innovative forest management techniques have been developed and adopted. In appropriate areas, helicopter logging is now used, allowing careful selection and removal of trees while limiting soil erosion, disruption to harvest sites, and the expense of building and maintaining logging roads. The impression of an unaltered landscape, particularly important to coastal ecotourism and sport fishing operators, is considered before harvesting coastline sites. Harvesting on steep slopes is restricted, and road-building standards have been improved to avoid siltation of streams and preserve slope stability.

Use of forest management techniques such as preharvest planning, site preparation, reforestation, spacing and thinning of trees, weeding, and fertilization of harvested areas has increased substantially. Planning and initiation of silvicultural techniques

TOP William Martin constructs a traditional dugout canoe from western redcedar, Tofino, Vancouver Island.

BOTTOM Prehistoric petroglyphs, Sproat Lake Provincial Park, Vancouver Island.

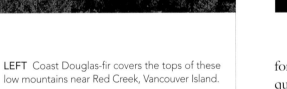

LEFT Coast Douglas-fir covers the tops of these low mountains near Red Creek, Vancouver Island.

RIGHT In some areas of the coastal forest, helicopters haul logs to minimize the environmental impacts of harvesting.

for a given site is based on consideration of a wide range of factors that include soil quality, hydrology, ecology, biodiversity, economic potential, wildlife habitat qualities, and potential for recreational use.

The coastal forest contains some of the oldest and largest trees in Canada. Trees older than 250 years are considered to be old growth, and such trees constitute 55% of the coastal forest, or 40 959 km^2. Other recognized qualities of old-growth forest are a complex mixture of tree species of varying size and age, frequent dead standing trees that create habitat for wildlife, and a thick lichen, moss, and shrub understory.

Great concern has been generated worldwide regarding forest management practices and the need to preserve old-growth ecosystems. Protected areas, including large sections of the central portion of the forest, have been established to conserve rain forest ecosystems, wildlife habitat, and other ecological values. Increasingly, harvesting in the coastal forest takes place in second-growth forests. Where harvesting continues in old-growth forests, forest practice codes require retention of an appropriate amount

of old growth across the landscape. Forest companies, conservation groups, Aboriginal peoples, and government work together to develop land-use plans and special management techniques to conserve habitat for species such as the grizzly bear, spotted owl, and marbled murrelet, each of which depends on old growth.

The coastal forest contains many national and provincial parks: for example, Gwaii Haanas National Park Reserve and Haida Heritage Site; Pacific Rim National Park Reserve; Kluane National Park and Reserve; and Flores Island, Skookumchuck Narrows, Cape Scott, Mount Seymour, and Indian Arm provincial parks.

The towering trees, unique ecosystems, productive forests, and extensive untouched wilderness areas of the coastal forest are to many around the world the very image and embodiment of Canada. Maintaining the health, biodiversity, and productivity of this forest is a global responsibility and one to which Canada is fully dedicated. To Canadians, the coastal forest is a national treasure and an opportunity to demonstrate forest stewardship to the world.

Coast Mountains along Howe Sound, near Horseshoe Bay.

TOP Wind storms brought down these large Douglas-firs in Cathedral Grove near Port Alberni.

BOTTOM In the shadow of tall trees, mosses and fungi thrive.

RIGHT A matched pair of mature bigleaf maples.

The largest standing Douglas-fir in Canada, the 73.8-m Red Creek Fir, has been growing for close to a thousand years near Port Renfrew, Vancouver Island.

URBAN
FOREST

Canada's urban forest is, like its natural counterparts,
both complex and dynamic

From its historical origins as a distant colony with a tiny and dispersed rural population, Canada has evolved into a country described by the Organization for Economic Cooperation and Development as one of the most urbanized nations on earth. The majority of Canadians (79.4% as of 2001) live in urban centers of 10 000 people or more; half (51%) are concentrated into four regions: southern Ontario; Montréal and surrounding areas in Quebec; southern Vancouver Island and the British Columbia lower mainland; and the corridor between Calgary and Edmonton, Alberta. The populations of these four regions grew by 7.6% between 1996 and 2001, while in the rest of the country, there was little or no population growth.

Although Canada's population is largely urban, public concern for the health and sustainability of forest resources has never been greater. Public demands for increased protection of forests and for pursuit of nature-related activities have increased, even as daily contact with natural forests has diminished. In southern Ontario,

84% of urban residents surveyed[1] said the presence of trees in the local community and of woodlots and forests in the surrounding regions was important. Most thought trees were essential in helping to improve air quality, and 68% visited forests or other natural areas in their city more than once a month.

Canada's urban landscape comprises 0.2% of the Canadian landmass and is estimated to be 19% forest. The urban forest overlaps with the ranges of many of Canada's species of special concern and is 85–90% privately owned. Edmonton, Alberta, a mid-sized urban center, has 103 000 trees on boulevards and 142 000 trees in parks, with an estimated value in excess of $800 million. Toronto, Canada's largest

Planted little-leaf lindens form a canopy along University Avenue, Toronto, Ontario.

[1] Environics Research Group. 2001. Attitudes of urban residents toward urban forests and woodlands issues. Prepared for the Ontario Ministry of the Environment, the Federation of Ontario Naturalists, Ontario Stewardship, and the Regional Municipality of York. 11 p.

TOP Flowering cherries on Belmont Avenue, Vancouver, British Columbia.

BOTTOM Ottawa's street trees are an integral part of the holiday season.

RIGHT Vancouver's Stanley Park, a coastal forest within the city.

urban center, has about 469 450 trees on streets, 2.5 million trees in parks and ravines, and another 2.5 million on private property.

Precise definition of the urban forest depends on perspective. While it begins with the individual trees that line city streets, most Canadian cities include significant parts of natural forest inherited from the rural landscape. Remnant forest stands, wooded river valleys, cemeteries, and parks are often found within urban boundaries. The Professional Foresters Act of Ontario, drafted in 2000, broadly defines the urban forest as "tree-dominated vegetation and related features found within an urban area, including woodlots, plantations, shade trees, street trees, fields in various stages of succession, wetlands, grassland corridors and riparian areas."

The definition of an urban forest can be expanded to include all natural areas into which urban Canadians extend an influence, particularly the places where they pass leisure time. By this definition, the urban forest radiates out into and links the space between cities, taking in satellite communities, conservation areas, provincial parks, and cottage country. Like Canada's natural forests, the urban forest is complex, diverse, and dynamic.

However defined, the urban forest provides numerous benefits to Canadians. The urban forest improves air quality by sequestering gaseous air pollutants and airborne particulates. Because they are often located in industrialized areas, urban trees are considered 5–15 times more beneficial than wilderness trees for reducing air pollution. They lower ambient temperatures by shading concrete surfaces and by excreting water vapor into the atmosphere. Urban trees contribute to energy conservation by shading and sheltering buildings, thereby reducing the demand for air conditioning in summer and for heating in winter. The urban forest buffers cities during weather events, reduces storm water runoff, controls soil erosion, and reduces noise pollution. It provides habitat for wildlife that otherwise could not survive in altered and highly populated areas.

The urban forest contributes directly to the physiological well-being and quality of life of Canadians. As it develops and ages, it is part of the heritage and identity of city landscapes. The urban forest increases real estate values. Winnipeg's approximately 62 225 boulevard elm trees are estimated to be worth $307 144 860 and contribute an estimated $160 000 000 to property values. In Toronto, a single premium mature tree may be valued at over $10 000. By improving the aesthetics of communities and individual properties, the urban forest attracts business activity and generates income. It provides a crucial link and gives context to broader environmental concerns and issues that exist beyond the immediate urban community. More than mere landscape, the urban forest functions as green infrastructure, providing natural services to city dwellers.

Canada's urban forest combines careful horticultural design with spontaneous natural growth. Typically, it includes native and introduced tree species, which are chosen for their hardiness, as measured by several climatic factors.

In eastern Canada, the urban landscape often includes native species such as white spruce, red oak, and silver maple, interspersed with the introduced Norway maple,

In Canada, municipalities manage urban forest resources. Most policies, regulations, laws, and other instruments that govern the sustainable management of urban forests have been enacted at the municipal level.

Urban foresters face the same challenges and seek the same kinds of information as do their natural forest counterparts. Many of the species found in Canadian broadleaf and coniferous forests also occur on the lawns, along the city streets, and in the parks and greenbelts of urban Canada. Knowledge on forest insect pests, tree diseases, remote-sensing methodologies, and invasive alien species is thus required by urban foresters to protect this valuable forest.

English oak, Austrian pine, little-leaf linden, and Russian-olive. In central Canada, a cold, dry prairie climate demands hardy, stress-tolerant native species such as trembling aspen, balsam poplar, plains cottonwood, green ash, and choke cherry, and introduced species such as Colorado spruce, European mountain-ash, and Amur maple. Streets in the cities of lower mainland British Columbia might feature all of the above trees, supplemented by monkey-puzzle from South America, umbrella-pines from Japan, Sierra redwoods from California, and tulip-trees from southern Ontario. Whatever the source, to succeed in an urban forest, tree species must be survivors. Air pollution, summer heat, drought, compacted soil, overcrowding, and road salt limit growth and shorten the lives of urban trees. Climatic extremes, including drought and fluctuating temperatures, are often reported as the greatest challenge in managing urban forest health.

A specialized branch of forest management, urban forestry, has evolved to meet the complex requirements of preserving and protecting the urban landscape. In

Place d'Armes on a winter's evening, Québec City, Quebec.

The sun sets on a cyclist in Mount Douglas Park, Victoria, British Columbia.

Canada, its development can be traced to the 1960s and efforts taken to combat Dutch elm disease, caused by an introduced pathogen that has decimated elm species in urban and rural forests alike. Elms were the most prevalent street tree across most of Canada. Provincial forestry institutions and the federal government collaborated to seek ways to limit the loss of the stately elm from urban landscapes. In spite of this, white elm has largely disappeared from eastern Canadian cities. However, large populations are still found in the cities of western Canada—Winnipeg has more than 200 000 white elms and Edmonton more than 60 000.

Contemporary urban forestry has evolved into a broader, ecosystem-based discipline that includes all aspects of planning, designing, establishing, and managing forests for economic, environmental, and social benefits. Today's urban forester might be involved in any number of activities, from the maintenance of a heritage forest to reestablishing forest cover lost to urban growth or even installing forest cover where none existed previously.

Canada's urban forest is on the frontline in the battle with invasive alien species. International ports in large cities are the primary arrival sites of alien insects and diseases in Canada. As a result, the urban forest has become the initial point of establishment for many of them. Examples of this include the discovery of brown spruce longhorn beetle in a Halifax, Nova Scotia, park; emerald ash borer in Windsor, Ontario, street trees; and numerous temperate and subtropical alien insects in Vancouver, British Columbia, landfill sites. Once established, invasive alien species are capable of migrating from the urban forest to the extensive natural forests beyond. The threat of these introductions into the urban forest is increasing.

At the outer edges of the urban forest, sugar bushes, fruit and nut tree orchards, Christmas tree farms, shelterbelts, and reforestation projects add another dimension to the relationship Canadians have with forests. Historically, tree plantations were established in Canada to fight soil erosion and to reclaim abandoned or marginal farmland. Now they are purpose-designed forest landscapes that involve farming

TOP Cross-country ski training in Odell Park, Fredericton, New Brunswick.

BOTTOM Skateboarding on the Fortune Parkway, Gatineau Park, Quebec.

LEFT Black walnut grove planted in 1882, Domaine Joly-De Lotbinière, Sainte-Croix, Quebec.

TOP   An urban forest landscape in the town of Simcoe, Ontario.

BOTTOM   Forest and gardens of Domaine de Maizerets, Québec City, Quebec.

RIGHT   Ornamentals, Colorado spruce (left) and Camperdown elm (right), in the Fredericton Botanic Garden, New Brunswick.

with high-yield species of trees. As the global demand for forest products increases— a trend projected to continue throughout the twenty-first century—high-yield forest plantations could provide Canada with an important new source of wood fiber. Such a supply would allow Canada to remain competitive in global markets without placing additional production pressure on natural forests. Large-scale forest plantations might also be a source of material for alternative fuels and a means of removing and storing carbon from the earth's atmosphere.

Canada's urban forest, though limited in extent, is significant as a national resource. Canadians create and sustain this valuable forest, and through it connect with the extensive natural forests that lie beyond.

TOP Nikka Yuko Japanese Garden, Lethbridge, Alberta.

BOTTOM Golfing in Fundy National Park, New Brunswick.

SOURCES

ELECTRONIC AND PRINT PUBLICATIONS

American Ornithologists' Union (AOU), The Committee on Classification and Nomenclature. 1998. *Checklist of North American Birds.* 7th ed. AOU, Washington, D.C.

Atlantic Geoscience Society. 2001. *The Last Billion Years: A Geological History of the Maritime Provinces of Canada.* Nimbus Publishing/Atlantic Geoscience Society, Halifax, NS.

Bailey, L.H.; Bailey, E.Z. 1976. *Hortus Third.* Macmillan Publishing Co., New York.

Brayshaw, T.C. 1996. *Trees and Shrubs of British Columbia.* Royal British Columbia Museum, Victoria, BC/UBC Press, Vancouver, BC.

Brodo, I.M.; Duran Sharnoff, S.; Sharnoff, S. 2001. *Lichens of North America.* Yale University Press, New Haven, MA, in collaboration with the Canadian Museum of Nature, Ottawa. 828 p.

Burns, R. M.; Honkala, B.H. Technical coordinators. 1990. *Silvics of North America*: 1. *Conifers*; 2. *Hardwoods.* Print and online. U.S. Department of Agriculture, Forest Service, Washington, DC. Agriculture Handbook 654. http://www.na.fs.fed.us/spfo/pubs/silvics_manual/table_of_contents.htm

Calder, J.A.; Taylor, R.L. 1968. *Flora of the Queen Charlotte Islands.* Part 1. *Systematics of the Vascular Plants.* Agriculture Canada, Research Branch, Ottawa, ON. Monograph 4.

Cody, J.W.; Britton, D.M. 1989. *Ferns and Fern Allies of Canada.* Department of Agriculture, Research Branch, Ottawa, ON. Publication 1829/E.

Darbyshire, S.J.; Favreau, M.; Murray, M. 2000. *Common and scientific names of weeds in Canada.* Agriculture and Agri-Food Canada, Research Branch. Publication 1397/B.132 p.

Drushka, K.; Burt, B. 2001 The Canadian Forest Service: catalyst for the forest sector. *Forest History Today* (Spring/Fall): 19–28.

Drushka, K.; Konttinen, H. 1997. *Tracks in the Forest: The Evolution of Logging Machinery.* Timberjack Group, Helsinki, Finland.

Ecological Stratification Working Group. 1996. *A National Ecological Framework for Canada.* Print and online. Agriculture and Agri-Food Canada, Research Branch, Ottawa, ON/Environment Canada, Ecozone Analysis Branch, Hull, QC. http://sis.agr.gc.ca/cansis/publications/ecostrat/intro.html

Gartshore, M.E.; Sutherland, D.A.; McCracken, J.D. 1987. *Haldimand-Norfolk Natural Areas Inventory.* 2 vols. Norfolk Field Naturalists, Simcoe, ON. 500 p.

Gray, S.L. 1995. *A Descriptive Forest Inventory of Canada's Forest Regions.* Natural Resources Canada, Canadian Forest Service, Petawawa National Forestry Institute, Chalk River, ON. Information Report PI-X-122.

Hebda, R. 1995. *Native Plants of British Columbia.* Online. Royal British Columbia Museum, Victoria, BC. Articles originally published in the *Coastal Grower.* http://rbcm1.rbcm.gov.bc.ca/nh_papers/nativeplants/index.html

Hydro-Québec. 1998. Répertoire des arbres et arbustes ornementaux. 2nd edition. Hydro-Québec, Montréal, QC.

Johnstone, K. 1991. *Timber and Trauma: 75 Years with the Federal Forestry Service, 1899–1974.* Forestry Canada, Ottawa. 194 p.

LandOwner Resource Centre.1999. Restoring old growth features to managed forests in southern Ontario. *Extension Notes.* LandOwner Resource Centre, Manotick, ON. 8 p.

Larson, B.M.; Riley, J.L.; Snell, E.A.; Godschalk, H.G. 1999. *The Woodland Heritage of Southern Ontario: A Study of Ecological Change, Distribution and Significance.* Federation of Ontario Naturalists, Don Mills, ON.

Lower, A.R.M. 1938. *The North American Assault on the Canadian Forest: A History of the Lumber Trade between Canada and the United States.* Ryerson Press, Toronto.

Lynch, W. 2001. *The Great Northern Kingdom: Life in the Boreal Forest.* Fitzhenry and Whiteside Limited, Markham, ON. 160 p.

Lyons, C.P. 1991. *Trees, Shrubs and Flowers to Know in British Columbia.* Fitzhenry and Whiteside Limited, Markham, ON.

MacKay, D. 1978. *The Lumberjacks.* McGraw-Hill Ryerson Limited, Toronto, ON.

Meidinger, D.; Pojar, J. Editors. 1991. *Ecosystems of British Columbia.* British Columbia Ministry of Forests, Research Branch. Special Report Series 6. 330 p.

Montpellier, P. 1999. City of the Month—Vancouver, British Columbia. Print and online. *City Trees: Journal of the Society of Municipal Arborists* 35(2: March/April). http://www.urban-forestry.com/citytrees/ v35n2a04.html

Natural Resources Canada (NRCan), Canadian Forest Service (CFS). 2002. *Canada's Forest Biodiversity. A Decade of Progress in Sustainable Forest Management.* Science Branch, NRCan, CFS, Ottawa. 58 p.

Natural Resources Canada (NRCan), Canadian Forest Service (CFS). 2002. *The State of Canada's Forests 2001–2002: Reflections of a Decade.* NRCan, CFS, Ottawa.

Nowak, R.M. 1999. *Walker's Mammals of the World.* 6th ed. Vols. 1 and 2. The Johns Hopkins University Press, Baltimore, MD.

Oliver, C.D.; Larson, B.C. *Forest Stand Dynamics.* McGraw-Hill, Inc., New York.

Ontario Ministry of Natural Resources (OMNR). 1997/1998. *A Silvicultural Guide for the Great Lakes–St. Lawrence Conifer Forest in Ontario.* Print and online. OMNR, Toronto. 424 p. http://www.mnr.gov.on.ca/MNR/forests/forestdoc/guidelines/grt%20lks/pdf/toc.pdf

Ontario Ministry of Natural Resources (OMNR). 1997/1998. *A Silvicultural Guide for the Tolerant Hardwood Forest in Ontario.* Print and online. OMNR, Toronto. 500 p. http://www.mnr.gov.on.ca/MNR/forests/forestdoc/guidelines/hrdwd/pdf/sec1.pdf

Ontario Ministry of Natural Resources (OMNR). 1997. *Silvicultural Guide to Managing for Black Spruce, Jack Pine and Aspen on Boreal Forest Ecosites in Ontario.* Version 1.1. OMNR, Toronto. 3 books. 822 p.

Peattie, D.C. 1948. *A Natural History of Trees of Eastern and Central North America.* Introduction by R. Finch, 1991. Houghton Mifflin Co., Boston.

Ringius; G.S.; Sims, R.A. 1997. *Indicator Plant Species in Canadian Forests*. Natural Resources Canada, Canadian Forest Service, Ottawa, ON.

Ritchie, J.C. 1987. *Postglacial Vegetation of Canada*. Cambridge University Press, Cambridge, UK.

Roland, A.E.; Smith, E.C. 1969. *Flora of Nova Scotia*. Nova Scotia Museum, Halifax, NS. Reprinted from Proceedings of the Nova Scotia Institute of Science, vol. 26.

Rowe, J.S. 1972. *Forest Regions of Canada*. Department of the Environment, Canadian Forestry Service, Ottawa, ON.

Schellhaas, S.; Spurbeck, D.; Ohlson, P.; Keenum, D.; Riesterer, H. 2001. *Fire Disturbance Effects in Subalpine Forests of North Central Washington*. Online. US Department of Agriculture, Forest Service. http://www.fs.fed.us/pnw/pubs/journals/Subalpine.pdf

Scoggan, H.J. 1978. *The Flora of Canada*. 4 vols. National Museums of Canada, Ottawa, ON.

Soper, J.H.; Heimburger, M.L. 1985. *Shrubs of Ontario*. Royal Ontario Museum, Toronto, ON.

West, B. 1974. *The Firebirds: How Bush Flying Won Its Wings*. Ministry of Natural Resources, Toronto, ON.

WEB SITES

Note: All sites were consulted between April 2002 and May 2003. Links were verified for all sites in June 2003.

The Acadian Forest Region
http://www.web.net/~ccnb/forest/acadian/ac_index.htm
Conservation Council of New Brunswick

Alternatives to Conventional Clearcutting
http://www.for.gov.bc.ca/hfp/pubs/standman/atcc/atcc.htm
British Columbia Ministry of Forests, Forest Practices Branch

Atlas of Canada: Facts about Canada
http://atlas.gc.ca/site/english/facts/surfareas.html
Natural Resources Canada

BC Parks Info Centre
http://wlapwww.gov.bc.ca/bcparks/infocentre.htm
British Columbia Ministry of Water, Land and Air Protection

The Boreal Ecosystem
http://www.mb.ec.gc.ca/nature/ecosystems/da00s02.en.html
Environment Canada

Canada's First Nations: Migration Theories
http://www.ucalgary.ca/applied_history/tutor/firstnations/theories.html
University of Calgary/ Red Deer College/ The Applied History Research Group

Canadian Amphibian and Reptile Conservation Network
http://www.carcnet.ca/
Environment Canada, Ecological Monitoring and Assessment Network Coordinating Office, Ecosystem Science Directorate

Canadian Biodiversity Web Site
http://www.canadianbiodiversity.mcgill.ca/english/index.htm
Hosted by McGill University Faculty of Science

Canadian Geographic Information Systems: Land Capability for Forestry
http://geogratis.cgdi.gc.ca/clf/en
Natural Resources Canada

Canadian Geographical Names Database: Querying Geographical Names
http://geonames.nrcan.gc.ca/search/search_e.php
Geographical Names Board of Canada (GNBC) and Natural Resources Canada, Centre for Topographic Information

Canadian Model Forest Network
http://www.modelforest.net/e/home_/indexe.html

Carolinian Canada
http://www.carolinian.org/

Centres of Plant Diversity: The Americas
http://www.nmnh.si.edu/botany/projects/cpd/na/na.htm
Smithsonian Institution, Department of Systematic Biology

Committee on the Status of Endangered Wildlife in Canada (COSEWIC)
http://www.cosewic.gc.ca/index.htm
Hosted by Environment Canada

Community Development: Montane Subregion
http://www.cd.gov.ab.ca/preserving/parks/anhic/montane.asp
Alberta Natural Heritage Information Centre, Government of Alberta

Directory of Research in the Wet Belt Forests in the Kamloops Forest Region
http://www.for.gov.bc.ca/kamloops/research/wetbelt/
British Columbia Ministry of Forests

Dutch Elm Disease Program
http://www.city.winnipeg.mb.ca/pwdforestry/dedweb2.html
City of Winnipeg

Ecological Subregions of the United States
http://www.fs.fed.us/land/pubs/ecoregions/
US Department of Agriculture, Forest Service

Ecosystems Management Emulating Natural Disturbance
http://www.biology.ualberta.ca/old_site/emend//english/homepage_e.html
Hosted by the University of Alberta

Edmonton Tree Facts
http://www.gov.edmonton.ab.ca/comm_services/parkland_services/forestry/edmonton_tree_facts.html
City of Edmonton

Environmental Stewardship: The Status of Western Red Cedar in Coastal British Columbia.
http://www.weyerhaeuser.com/coastalwood/wycedar/cedar_environ.htm.
Weyerhaeuser

Fire Effects Information System: Plant Species Summaries
http://www.fs.fed.us/database/feis/index.html
US Department of Agriculture, Forest Service

First Nations Forestry Program
http://www.fnfp.gc.ca/
Government of Canada

Flora of North America
http://hua.huh.harvard.edu/FNA/index.html

The Forest Resources of Ontario 1996
http://www.mnr.gov.on.ca/MNR/forests/fmb_info/html
Ontario Ministry of Natural Resources

Forest Stewardship Council of Canada: Draft Standards
http://www.web.net/fscca/stancon.htm

Forestry Branch Services
http://www.winnipeg.ca/publicworks/Forestry/forestry.asp
City of Winnipeg

Forestry: Planted Forests
http://www.fao.org/forestry/index.jsp
Food and Agriculture Organization of the United Nations

Fundy Model Forest
http://www.fundymodelforest.net/site/
Model Forest Network

General Description of the Prince Edward
Island Map Sheet Area
http://geogratis.cgdi.gc.ca/CLI/mapping/
descriptions/pei.html
Natural Resources Canada, Canada
Land Inventory

Global Atlas of Palaeovegetation since the
Last Glacial Maximum
http://www.soton.ac.uk/~tjms/adams4.html
Quaternary Environments Network

Great Lakes Ecological Assessment
http://www.ncrs.fs.fed.us/gla/histveg/
purpose.htm
US Department of Agriculture, Forest
Service

Integrated Taxonomic Information System
(ITIS)—North America
http://sis.agr.gc.ca/pls/itisca/taxaget?p_
ifx=plglt

John Prince Research Forest: Research
http://researchforest.unbc.ca/jprf/jprf.htm
University of Northern British Columbia/
Tl'azt'en First Nation

Kananaskis Field Stations: Research Activities
http://www.ucalgary.ca/UofC/research/KFS/
index.html
University of Calgary

1995 Land Cover of Canada
http://www.ccrs.nrcan.gc.ca/ccrs/rd/apps
/landcov/cchange/land_e.html
Natural Resources Canada, Canada
Centre for Remote Sensing

Long Point Region Conservation Authority:
Parks and Conservation Areas
http://www.lprca.on.ca/

Morris Tract
http://www.ontarioparks.com/english/
morr.html
Ontario Parks

Narrative Descriptions of Terrestrial
Ecozones and Ecoregions of Canada
http://www.ec.gc.ca/soer-ree/English/
Framework/NarDesc/TOC.cfm
Environment Canada

National Forest Information System
http://www.nfis.org/
Canadian Council of Forest Ministers

National Forestry Database Program:
Compendium of Canadian Forestry
Statistics
http://nfdp.ccfm.org/
Canadian Council of Forest Ministers

Natural Heritage: Carolinian Canada
http://www.heritagefdn.on.ca/Eng/Heritage/
natural-carolinian.shtml
Ontario Heritage Foundation

The Natural History of Nova Scotia
http://museum.gov.ns.ca/mnh/nature/nhns/
index.htm
Nova Scotia Museum of Natural History

A Profile of the Canadian Population: Highlights
from the 2001 Census of Population
http://geodepot.statcan.ca/Diss/Highlights/
Index_e.cfm
Statistics Canada

Research Areas—National Portals
http://www.nrcan.gc.ca/cfs-scf/science/
resrch/index_e.html
Natural Resources Canada, Canadian
Forest Service

Saskatchewan Dutch Elm Disease Association
http://www.sdeda.ca/

Sicamous Creek Silvicultural Systems Research
Project 1992–2001
http://www.mountainforests.net/sicamous/
siccreek.asp

South Okanagan Species at Risk
http://wlapwww.gov.bc.ca/sir/fwh/wld/atlas/
about/redbluelist.html
Government of British Columbia

Statistics on Natural Resources
http://www.nrcan.gc.ca/statistics/intro_e.html
Natural Resources Canada

Subalpine Forests
http://www.for.gov.bc.ca/hre/subalpin/
index.htm
British Columbia Ministry of Forests,
Research Branch

Tallgrass Ontario
http://www.tallgrassontario.org/

Urban Forest Health Care
http://www.toronto.ca/trees/forest_
healthcare.htm
City of Toronto

Urban Forestry
http://www.treecanada.ca/programs/
urbanforestry/index.htm
Tree Canada Foundation

The Vancouver Park Board's Street Tree
Management Program
http://www.city.vancouver.bc.ca/parks/fyi/
trees/treebro1.htm
City of Vancouver

SCIENTIFIC NAMES OF ORGANISMS

Acadian flycatcher, *Empidonax virescens*
alternate-leaf dogwood, *Cornus alternifolia*
amabilis fir, *Abies amabilis*
American badger, *Taxidea taxus*
American beaver, *Castor canadensis*
American beech, *Fagus grandifolia*
American black bear, *Ursus americanus*
American chestnut, *Castanea dentata*
American elder, *Sambucus canadensis*
American ginseng, *Panax quinquefolius*
American golden-plover, *Pluvialis dominica*
American pine marten, *Martes americana*
American pipit, *Anthus rubescens*
American sycamore, *Platanus occidentalis*
American twinflower, *Linnaea borealis*
Amur maple, *Acer ginnala*
antelope bitterbrush, *Purshia tridentata*
arbutus, *Arbutus menziesii*
armillaria root disease, *Armillaria ostoyae*
    (causative agent)
Austrian pine, *Pinus nigra*

bald eagle, *Haliaeetus leucocephalus*
balsam fir, *Abies balsamea*
balsam poplar, *Populus balsamifera*
bark beetles, Scolytidae
barred owl, *Strix varia*
basswood, *Tilia americana*
bay-breasted warbler, *Dendroica castanea*
beaked hazel, *Corylus cornuta*
Bebb willow, *Salix bebbiana*
big bluestem, *Andropogon gerardii*
bighorn sheep, *Ovis canadensis*
bigleaf maple, *Acer macrophyllum*
bitter cherry, *Prunus emarginata*
bitternut hickory, *Carya cordiformis*
black ash, *Fraxinus nigra*
black-capped chickadee, *Poecile atricapillus*
black cherry, *Prunus serotina*
black cottonwood, *Populus trichocarpa*
black huckleberry, *Gaylussacia baccata*
black oak, *Quercus velutina*
black oystercatcher, *Haematopus bachmani*
black spruce, *Picea mariana*
black tupelo (or black-gum), *Nyssa sylvatica*
black walnut, *Juglans nigra*
black willow, *Salix nigra*
Blanding's turtle, *Emydoidea blandingii*
blue ash, *Fraxinus quadrangulata*
blueberry, *Vaccinium* spp.
blue-berry elder, *Sambucus cerulea*

bluebunch wheatgrass, *Pseudoroegneria spicata*
    subsp. *spicata*
blue-gray gnatcatcher, *Polioptila caerulea*
bluejoint reedgrass, *Calamagrostis canadensis*
blue-spotted salamander, *Ambystoma laterale*
bobcat, *Lynx rufus*
bog Labrador-tea, *Ledum groenlandicum*
bog-laurel, *Kalmia polifolia*
boreal chickadee, *Poecile hudsonicus*
boreal chorus frog, *Pseudacris maculata*
bride's-bonnet, *Clintonia uniflora*
British Columbia wild-ginger, *Asarum caudatum*
brown spruce longhorn beetle, *Tetropium*
    fuscum
brown widelip orchid, *Liparis liliifolia*
bullfrog, *Rana catesbeiana*
bur oak, *Quercus macrocarpa*
burning-bush euonymus, *Euonymus*
    atropurpureus
burrowing owl, *Athene cunicularia*
butternut, *Juglans cinerea*
butternut canker, *Sirococcus clavigignenti-*
    juglandacearum (causative agent)

California quail, *Callipepla californica*
Camperdown elm, cultivar of Scotch elm, *Ulmus*
    glabra
Canada lily, *Lilium canadense*
Canada lynx, *Felis canadensis*
Canada mayflower, *Maianthemum canadense*
Canada plum, *Prunus nigra*
Canada yew, *Taxus canadensis*
Canadian bunchberry, *Cornus canadensis*
caribou, *Rangifer tarandus*
Carolina wren, *Thryothorus ludovicianus*
cascade azalea, *Rhododendron albiflorum*
cascara buckthorn, *Rhamnus purshiana*
cherries, *Prunus* sp.
chestnut-backed chickadee, *Poecile rufescens*
chinook salmon, *Oncorhynchus tshawytscha*
choke cherry, *Prunus virginiana* var. *virginiana*
chum salmon, *Oncorhynchus keta*
clouded salamander, *Aneides ferreus*
coast Douglas-fir, *Pseudotsuga menziesii* var.
    menziesii
coho salmon, *Oncorhynchus kisutch*
Colorado spruce, *Picea pungens*
Columbian ground squirrel, *Spermophilus*
    columbianus
Columbia spotted frog, *Rana luteiventris*
common buckeye butterfly, *Junonia coenia*

common garter snake, *Thamnophis sirtalis*
common hoptree, *Ptelea trifoliata*
common juniper, *Juniperus communis*
common snapping turtle, *Chelydra serpentina*
common winterberry, *Ilex verticillata*
common yarrow, *Achillea millefolium*
common yellow oxalis, *Oxalis stricta*
copperbush, *Elliottia pyroliflorus*
cottonwood, *Populus deltoides*
coyote, *Canis latrans*
cranberry, *Vaccinium* spp.
creeping juniper, *Juniperus horizontalis*
cucumber magnolia (or cucumber-tree),
    Magnolia acuminata

deer mouse, *Peromyscus maniculatus*
devil's-club, *Oplopanax horridus*
devil's-tongue (prickly-pear), *Opuntia humifusa*
dicranum moss, *Dicranum scoparium*
dogtooth violet, *Erythronium americanum*
Douglas-fir. *See* coast Douglas-fir *and* Rocky
    Mountain Douglas-fir
Douglas maple, *Acer glabrum* var. *douglasii*
dwarf birch, *Betula glandulosa*
dwarf chinquapin oak, *Quercus prinoides*
dwarf mistletoe, *Arceuthobium* spp.

eastern flowering dogwood, *Cornus florida*
eastern fox snake, *Elaphe vulpina gloydi*
eastern grasswort, *Lilaeopsis chinensis*
eastern hemlock, *Tsuga canadensis*
eastern leatherwood, *Dirca palustris*
eastern massasauga rattlesnake, *Sistrurus*
    catenatus catenatus
eastern milk snake, *Lampropeltis triangulum*
    triangulum
eastern painted turtle, *Chrysemys picta picta*
eastern redcedar, *Juniperus virginiana*
eastern ribbon snake, *Thamnophis sauritus*
eastern white-cedar, *Thuja occidentalis*
eastern white pine, *Pinus strobus*
emerald ash borer, *Agrilis planipennis*
Engelmann spruce, *Picea engelmannii*
English oak, *Quercus robur*
European mountain-ash, *Sorbus aucuparia*

false Solomon's-seal, *Maianthemum racemosum*
fescues, *Festuca* spp.
fireweed, *Epilobium angustifolium*
fisher, *Martes pennanti*
five-lined skink, *Eumeces fasciatus*

flying squirrel, *Glaucomys volans*
foothill arnica, *Arnica fulgens*
Fowler's toad, *Bufo fowleri*
fox squirrel, *Sciurus niger*
fragrant bedstraw, *Galium triflorum*

Garry oak, *Quercus garryana*
giant swallowtail, *Papilio cresphontes*
goldencrest, *Lophiola aurea*
golden-crowned sparrow, *Zonotrichia atricapilla*
golden weeping willow, *Salix alba* var. *vitellina*
grand fir, *Abies grandis*
gray birch, *Betula populifolia*
gray jay, *Perisoreus canadensis*
gray rabbitbrush, *Chrysothamnus nauseosus*
gray treefrog, *Hyla versicolor*
gray wolf, *Canis lupus*
Great Basin spadefoot, *Spea intermontana*
great blue heron, *Ardea herodias*
great gray owl, *Strix nebulosa*
green alder, *Alnus viridis* subsp. *crispa*
green ash, *Fraxinus pennsylvanica* var. *subintegerrima*
green dog lichen, *Peltigera aphthosa*
grizzly bear, *Ursus arctos*
grouse whortleberry, *Vaccinium scoparium*
gypsy moth, *Lymantria dispar*
gyrfalcon, *Falco rusticolus*

hawkweed, *Hieracium* spp.
hawthorn, *Crataegus* spp.
heartleaf arnica, *Arnica cordifolia*
heartleaf foamflower, *Tiarella cordifolia*
heather, *Calluna vulgaris*
hoary marmot, *Marmota caligata*
hollyleaved barberry, *Mahonia aquifolium*
hooded warbler, *Wilsonia citrina*
Hooker's mountain avens, *Dryas octopetala* var. *hookeriana*

Indian-pipe, *Monotropa uniflora*
ironwood, *Ostrya virginiana*

jack pine, *Pinus banksiana*
Jefferson salamander, *Ambystoma jeffersonianum*
junegrass, *Koeleria macrantha*

Kentucky coffeetree, *Gymnocladus dioicus*
killer whale, *Orcinus orca*
kinnikinnick, *Arctostaphylos uva-ursi*

largetooth aspen, *Populus grandidentata*
lichens, Cladoniaceae
limber pine, *Pinus flexilis*
Lincoln's sparrow, *Melospiza lincolnii*
little bluestem, *Schizachyrium scoparium*
little brown bat, *Myotis lucifuga*
little-leaf linden, *Tilia cordata*

lodgepole pine, *Pinus contorta* var. *latifolia*
long-tailed vole, *Microtus longicaudus*
long-toed salamander, *Ambystoma macrodactylum*

marbled murrelet, *Brachyramphus marmoratus*
Menzie's pipsissewa (little prince's pine), *Chimaphila menziesii*
miner's-lettuce, *Claytonia perfoliata*
monkey-puzzle, *Araucaria araucana*
moose, *Alces alces*
mountain-ash, *Sorbus* sp.
mountain avens, *Geum peckii*
mountain chickadee, *Poecile gambeli*
mountain goat, *Oreamnos americanus*
mountain hemlock, *Tsuga mertensiana*
mountain maple, *Acer spicatum*
mountain paper birch, *Betula cordifolia*
mountain pine beetle, *Dendroctonus ponderosae*
mountain quail, *Oreortyx pictus*
mountain rough fescue, *Festuca altaica* subsp. *scabrella*
mudpuppy, *Necturus maculosus*
mule deer, *Odocoileus hemionus*
muskrat, *Ondatra zibethicus*

New Jersey rush, *Juncus caesariensis*
North American porcupine, *Erethizon dorsatum*
northern alligator lizard, *Elgaria coerulea*
northern bayberry, *Myrica pensylvanica*
northern bedstraw, *Galium boreale*
northern cricket frog, *Acris crepitans*
northern goshawk, *Accipiter gentilis*
northern leopard frog, *Rana pipiens*
northern meadowsweet, *Spiraea septentrionalis*
northern mockingbird, *Mimus polyglottos*
northern pygmy-owl, *Glaucidium gnoma*
northern water snake, *Nerodia sipedon*
northwestern crow, *Corvus caurinus*
northwestern garter snake, *Thamnophis ordinoides*
Norway maple, *Acer platanoides*

Ohio buckeye, *Aesculus glabra*
orchard oriole, *Icterus spurius*
Oregon boxleaf (or mountain lover), *Paxistima myrsinites*
oval-leaf blueberry, *Vaccinium ovalifolium*

Pacific chorus frog, *Pseudacris regilla*
Pacific giant salamander, *Dicamptodon tenebrosus*
Pacific loon, *Gavia pacifica*
Pacific trillium, *Trillium ovatum*
Pacific willow, *Salix lucida* subsp. *lasiandra*
pawpaw, *Asimina triloba*
pileated woodpecker, *Dryocopus pileatus*

pinegrass, *Calamagrostis rubescens*
pine grosbeak, *Pinicola enucleator*
pine siskin, *Carduelis pinus*
pink salmon, *Oncorhynchus gorbuscha*
pink tickseed, *Coreopsis rosea*
pin oak, *Quercus palustris*
pitch pine, *Pinus rigida*
plains cottonwood, *Populus deltoides* ssp. *monilifera*
plains prickly-pear, *Opuntia polyacantha*
Plymouth rose gentian, *Sabatia kennedyana*
poison-ivy, *Toxicodendron radicans*
poison-oak, *Toxicodendron diversiloba*
poison-sumac, *Toxicodendron vernix*
ponderosa pine, *Pinus ponderosa*
poplar, *Populus* spp.
prairie sagewort, *Artemisia frigida*
pumpkin ash, *Fraxinus profunda*
purple pitcherplant, *Sarracenia purpurea*
pussy willow, *Salix discolor*

queen snake, *Regina septemvittata*

raccoon, *Procyon lotor*
ram's head lady's slipper, *Cypripedium arietinum*
red alder, *Alnus rubra*
red ash, *Fraxinus pennsylvanica* var. *pennsylvanica*
red-backed salamander, *Plethodon cinereus*
red-bellied woodpecker, *Melanerpes carolinus*
redbud, *Cercis canadensis*
red crossbill, *Loxia curvirostra*
red fox, *Vulpes vulpes*
red hickory, *Carya glabra* var. *odorata*
red huckleberry, *Vaccinium parvifolium*
red-legged frog, *Rana aurora*
red maple, *Acer rubrum*
red mulberry, *Morus rubra*
red oak, *Quercus rubra*
red-osier dogwood, *Cornus sericea*
red pine, *Pinus resinosa*
red-shouldered hawk, *Buteo lineatus*
red spruce, *Picea rubens*
red-tailed hawk, *Buteo jamaicensis*
red trillium, *Trillium erectum*
ringneck snake, *Diadophis punctatus*
river otter, *Lontra canadensis*
Rocky Mountain Douglas-fir, *Pseudotsuga menziesii* var. *glauca*
Rocky Mountain juniper, *Juniperus scopulorum*
Roemer's fescue, *Festuca roemeri*
root rot, *Armillaria* spp. (causative agent)
rose spirea, *Spiraea douglasii*
rough-legged hawk, *Buteo lagopus*
rough-skinned newt, *Taricha granulosa*
round-leaf dogwood, *Cornus rugosa*
round-leaf sundew, *Drosera rotundifolia*
rubber boa, *Charina bottae*

ruffed grouse, *Bonasa umbellus*
russet buffaloberry, *Shepherdia canadensis*
Russian-olive, *Elaeagnus angustifolia*
rusty menziesia, *Menziesia ferruginea*

sagebrush, *Artemisia* spp.
sage thrasher, *Oreoscoptes montanus*
salmonberry, *Rubus spectabilis*
Saskatoon-berry, *Amelanchier alnifolia*
sassafras, *Sassafras albidum*
Scots pine, *Pinus sylvestris*
scrub willow, *Salix* spp.
sea otter, *Enhydra lutris*
serviceberry, *Amelanchier* spp.
sharp-tailed snake, *Contia tenuis*
shellbark hickory, *Carya laciniosa*
shining willow, *Salix lucida* subsp. *lucida*
shore pine, *Pinus contorta* var. *contorta*
sideoats grama, *Bouteloua curtipendula*
Sierra redwood, *Sequoiadendron giganteum*
silky lupine, *Lupinus sericeus*
silver maple, *Acer saccharinum*
Sitka alder, *Alnus viridis* subsp. *sinuata*
Sitka spruce, *Picea sitchensis*
smooth blackberry, *Rubus canadensis*
smooth green snake, *Liochlorophis vernalis*
snowshoe hare, *Lepus americanus*
snow trillium, *Trillium grandiflorum*
snowy owl, *Nyctea scandiaca*
sockeye salmon, *Oncorhynchus nerka*
speckled alder, *Alnus incana* subsp. *rugosa*
sphagnum, *Sphagnum* spp.
spiny softshell turtle, *Apalone spinifera*
splendid feather moss, *Hylocomium splendens*
spotted frog, *Rana pretiosa*
spotted owl, *Strix occidentalis*
spotted turtle, *Clemmys guttata*
spreading phlox, *Phlox diffusa*
spring peeper, *Pseudacris crucifer*
spruce grouse, *Falcipennis canadensis*
squashberry viburnum, *Viburnum edule*

staghorn sumac, *Rhus typhina*
Steller's jay, *Cyanocitta stelleri*
striped maple, *Acer pensylvanicum*
subalpine fir, *Abies lasiocarpa*
subalpine larch, *Larix lyallii*
sugar maple, *Acer saccharum*
swamp white oak, *Quercus bicolor*
sweet fern, *Comptonia peregrina*
sweet pepperbush, *Clethra alnifolia*
sweet viburnum, *Viburnum lentago*

tailed frog, *Ascaphus truei*
tall cotton-grass, *Eriophorum angustifolium*
tamarack, *Larix laricina*
thimbleberry, *Rubus parviflorus*
thinleaf huckleberry, *Vaccinium membranaceum*
threadleaf sundew, *Drosera filiformis*
three birds orchid, *Triphora trianthophora*
three-toed woodpecker, *Picoides tridactylus*
tiger salamander, *Ambystoma tigrinum*
trailing arbutus, *Epigaea repens*
trembling aspen, *Populus tremuloides*
tufted alpine saxifrage, *Saxifraga caespitosa*
tufted puffin, *Fratercula cirrhata*
tulip-tree, *Liriodendron tulipifera*

umbrella-pine, *Sciadopitys verticillata*

Virginia opossum, *Didelphis virginiana*
Virginia strawberry, *Fragaria virginiana*

wapiti, *Cervus elaphus*
water birch, *Betula occidentalis*
water pennywort, *Hydrocotyle umbellata*
western flowering dogwood, *Cornus nuttallii*
western gromwell, *Lithospermum ruderale*
western hemlock, *Tsuga heterophylla*
western larch, *Larix occidentalis*
western oak fern, *Gymnocarpium dryopteris*
    subsp. *disjunctum*
western painted turtle, *Chrysemys picta belli*

western rattlesnake, *Crotalus viridis*
western redcedar, *Thuja plicata*
western skink, *Eumeces skiltonianus*
western snowberry, *Symphoricarpos occidentalis*
western terrestrial garter snake, *Thamnophis elegans*
western toad, *Bufo boreas*
western white birch, *Betula papyrifera* var. *commutata*
western white pine, *Pinus monticola*
western yew, *Taxus brevifolia*
wheatgrass, *Agropyron* spp.
white ash, *Fraxinus americana*
whitebark pine, *Pinus albicaulis*
white birch, *Betula papyrifera*
white-breasted nuthatch, *Sitta carolinensis*
white elm, *Ulmus americana*
white-headed woodpecker, *Picoides albolarvatus*
white mulberry, *Morus alba*
white oak, *Quercus alba*
white pine blister rust, *Cronartium ribicola* (causative agent)
white spruce, *Picea glauca*
white-tailed deer, *Odocoileus virginianus*
white-tailed ptarmigan, *Lagopus leucurus*
white-throated sparrow, *Zonotrichia albicollis*
wild crab apple, *Malus coronaria*
wild leek, *Allium tricoccum*
wild sarsaparilla, *Aralia nudicaulis*
witch-hazel, *Hamamelis virginiana*
wood duck, *Aix sponsa*
wood frog, *Rana sylvatica*
woodland caribou, *Rangifer tarandus*
wood turtle, *Clemmys insculpta*

yellow-bellied sapsucker, *Sphyrapicus varius*
yellow birch, *Betula alleghaniensis*
yellow-breasted chat, *Icteria virens*
yellow-cedar, *Chamaecyparis nootkatensis*
yellow-pine chipmunk, *Tamias amoenus*
yellow skunk cabbage, *Lysichiton americanum*

ACKNOWLEDGMENTS

We wish to thank Canadian Forest Service (CFS), Natural Resources Canada, staff who reviewed portions of the manuscript: **Bob Burt**, **Ian D. Campbell**, **Jennifer Dunlap**, **Jacques Gagnon**, **Peter Hall**, **Yvan Hardy**, **Bradley Henry**, **Gordon Miller**, **David Tuck**, and **Maureen Whelan**, Headquarters (HQ), Ottawa; **Tom Murray**, **Janice Campbell**, and **Gerrit D. van Raalte**, Atlantic Forestry Centre (AFC), Fredericton, New Brunswick; **Ken Baldwin**, Great Lakes Forestry Centre (GLFC), Sault Ste. Marie, Ontario; and **Art Shortreid**, **Bill Wagner**, and **Roger Whitehead**, Pacific Forestry Centre (PFC), Victoria, British Columbia. Thanks also to **Michael Rosen** of the Tree Canada Foundation for review of the chapter describing urban forests.

The CFS Forests of Canada Working Group was composed of **Joseph Anawati**, **Jennifer Dunlap**, **Brian Haddon**, and **André Rousseau**, HQ; **Lynda Chambers**, PFC; **Russ Bohning**, Northern Forestry Centre (NFC), Edmonton, Alberta; **Pamela Cheers** and **Joan Murphy**, Laurentian Forestry Centre (LFC), Sainte-Foy, Quebec; **Guy Smith**, GLFC; and **Tom Murray**, AFC. Their advice at the inception phase of this project was invaluable. In addition, technical advice was generously given by **Bill Meades**, GLFC, and **Edward Szakowski** and **Jacques Trencia**, HQ.

Derek Sidders, NFC, and **Gaetan Pelletier**, Management Forester, J.D. Irving Limited, St. Leonard, New Brunswick, provided field assistance to photographer J. David Andrews. **Lizanne Gosselin**, Vancouver, British Columbia, assisted the author with location of urban shots. A special thank you to **Tom Murray**, AFC, and **Guy Smith**, GLFC, for research on location information for the project photographers. **Benoît Arsenault**, LFC, **Stéphane Leroy**, Director, Marketing, Amphibious Aircraft, Bombardier Aerospace, Montréal, Quebec, and **Debra Wortley**, Forest Management Branch, and **Rob Bales**, Department of Tourism and Culture, Yukon Territorial Government, Whitehorse, helped to locate archival photographs.

We also thank the following: **Josef Cihlar** and **Rasim Latifovic**, Natural Resources Canada, Canada Centre for Remote Sensing, Ottawa, for providing digital files of the Land Cover of Canada satellite data map, which was adapted for this publication; **Marc Favreau**, Translation Bureau, Public Works and Government Services Canada, Montréal, Quebec, for his support in translating the publication and whose botanical knowledge contributed to the quality of the publication in both languages; and **Jacques Gagnon**, Canadian Forest Service, Ottawa, for his expertise and energy during the initial and final phases of the project.

PHOTOGRAPH CREDITS

J. DAVID ANDREWS

p. 5; p. 10, bottom; p. 13; p. 16–35; p. 36, © J. David Andrews; p. 38–42; p. 43, left, © J. David Andrews; p. 43, right; p. 44–51; p. 54–55; p. 58, bottom; p. 60; p. 62–63; p. 64, top, © J. David Andrews; p. 66–67; p. 68, left; p. 71–84; p. 88; p. 90–91; p. 114–115; p. 130–133; p. 136–137; p. 139–141.

LENARD SANDERS

p. 6; p. 85–87; p. 89; p. 92–103; p. 105–113; p. 116, bottom; p. 117; p. 119–120; p. 122–125; p. 126, left; p. 128, top, bottom; p. 129, above; p. 138.

ROBERTA GAL

p. 10, top; p. 52–53, © Roberta Gal; p. 64, bottom; p. 104; p. 116, top; p. 118; p. 121; p. 127; p. 128, right; p. 134, top; p. 134, bottom, © Roberta Gal; p. 135.

DAVID BARBOUR

p. 56–57; p. 58, top; p. 59; p. 61; p. 65; p. 68, right; p. 69–70.

NATIONAL ARCHIVES OF CANADA

p. 8, National Archives of Canada, Ottawa (Accession No. R9266-278), Peter Winkworth Collection of Canadiana; p. 9, top, H. Peters, National Archives of Canada, PA-135750; p. 9, bottom, National Film Board of Canada, Photothèque/National Archives of Canada, PA-116932.

BOMBARDIER AEROSPACE

p. 11, © Bombardier Aerospace, photo by Cliff Symons.

GOVERNMENT OF YUKON

p. 37, © Government of Yukon, photo by Robin Armour.

INTERNATIONAL FOREST PRODUCTS LIMITED

p. 126, right, © International Forest Products Limited, photo by Katrina Sutcliffe.

INDEX